Glimpses of China

Ingrid Rogers

BRETHREN PRESS
Elgin, Illinois

Glimpses of China

Copyright © 1989 by Ingrid Rogers

BRETHREN PRESS, 1451 Dundee Avenue, Elgin, Illinois 60120

Cover design by Kathy Kline Miller

Library of Congress Cataloging in Publication Data
Rogers, Ingrid.
    Glimpses of China / Ingrid Rogers.
      p.   cm.
    ISBN 0-87178-317-7
    1. China—Description and travel—1976- 2. Rogers, Ingrid—
Journeys—China. I. Title.
    DS712.R63   1989
    915.1'0458—dc19   88-39447
                                                      CIP

Manufactured in the United States of America

Contents

Introduction. v
1. The First Glimpse 1
2. Some Cultural Differences 29
3. Observations. 53
4. Discoveries 63
5. Memories 79
6. Many-Splendored Things 101
7. Travel 111
8. A Last Look 125

Introduction

"How would you like to go to China?"

I looked at my husband in stunned surprise, trying to discern whether he was toying with an abstract idea or making a concrete proposal.

"Allen Deeter has asked us whether we want to be the first directors of the new program, beginning next February," Ken continued as if the news were a casual matter. I felt myself flushing, then paling with excitement, like a teenager who had just been asked for a date. China! Within a split second, dozens of images flashed through my mind: people in straw hats, wading in rice paddies; Mao statues and skirted roof tops; chopsticks, spices, and green tea; enchanting oriental music; and cryptic signs only Chinese people could read. I was drawn by an overwhelming curiosity. Something was in the making that would significantly change my life.

"I told him we probably couldn't go," Ken said, interrupting my brief daydream.

"You did what?"

Slowly, he brought me back to reality. "This whole academic year has already been planned, remember? I was counting on taking a group of students to Germany next May, and several people have already expressed interest in participating. All the courses at the college have been assigned. You are beginning your seminary studies in just a few weeks, and you have a church to pastor."

It was true. Everything considered, perhaps this was not the right time. But how could we pass up such an opportunity? And would there ever be a better time? Wasn't this significant enough to drop other considerations? China in a matter of minutes had become the place of my dreams, drawing me like a magnet. I felt an irresistible sense of calling that overrode any argument of inconvenience.

My passion for going abroad was not new. Curiosity about foreign countries and a longing to contribute to world peace and understanding had first brought me to the United States as an exchange student from Germany at age sixteen. I also had lived in France and England for extended periods of study—never just as a tourist, but as someone willing to stay a while, to learn the ways of the people.

For about a week, we talked of hardly anything besides the China prospects. Gradually, doors began to open. Ken's colleagues proved marvelously cooperative in their willingness to hire a part-time replacement and to redistribute the course load for the spring semester. The trip to Germany was easy to postpone. As for the seminary, I was majoring in Peace Studies, and what could be a more appropriate project than to help establish an international exchange program? My congregation caught the vision of a unique world ministry project; at the next church council meeting, they voted unanimously to send us with their blessing. An interim pastor was called to carry on ministerial duties during my absence, with the expectation that I would resume pastoring once we returned from China. The district held a commissioning service, a moving celebration assuring us of endorsement from the wider church.

During the few remaining months before the departure I prepared diligently for our overseas assignment. I read books and articles about China, corresponded with former missionaries, and contacted friends who had visited the country as tourists and were willing to show us slides. Nine Chinese exchange students and their teachers at Goshen College met with us to share about their country and their efforts at cross-cultural communication.

Despite these preparations, I continued to feel ignorant about Chinese society and about what would await us. But was my lack of expertise such a disadvantage? Perhaps a meaningful cultural interchange could still occur even though I went with more questions than answers. The real learning about China would happen when we lived there. I looked forward to letting the people of Dalian teach me about their homeland.

We went with the intention of entering the foreign culture as learners, and indeed, every day brought new opportunities for cross-cultural adventures. I relished them. Throughout our sojourn I remained eager to uncover China's secrets, to observe, evaluate, and seek to understand.

We assumed mutuality in our encounter with the Chinese people. The exchange program was set up in such a way that both sides participated equally. The American students taught English and learned Chinese; we came to Dalian while Chinese instructors went to college campuses in the United States; the host institutions on both sides supported the visitors financially and provided room and board.

We went to China with the understanding that establishing the exchange would be a peace mission. There are so many misconceived notions about China in the United States. While political relations have eased since the visit of President Nixon, the Asian country remains enigmatic and distant. My goal was not to return with facts and figures, but to seek ways to describe the Chinese people so that they would become less abstract. For me a peace-filled encounter with China required showing respect for the host culture, living as much as possible like the Chinese people do, actively seeking friendship with individual Chinese, and counteracting prejudices by writing about our adventures in a supportive and nonjudgmental way.

So I went to China wanting to learn, anticipating mutuality, and striving to build international bonds of peace. I am not sure I always succeeded. Having lived in China for six months, I knew I was *still* a novice about the country. My willingness to live like a Chinese person was thwarted by our hosts' gracious insistence on pampering foreigners with superior living conditions and "favors." Peacemaking efforts became secondary at times when tedious administrative regulations and immense cultural differences drove us to distraction. On the other hand, we had succeeded in building lasting friendships; we could look back on six months of ineradicable memories; and we were able to celebrate that for us and our new friends, the world had grown smaller.

From the beginning of our stay in Dalian, I kept a detailed journal. This helped my adjustment process in two ways. First of all, living in China meant having to absorb an abundance of impressions, some delightful, some repulsive, but all challenging because of the striking contrast to the West. The journal made it possible to take mental photographs—to verbalize my initial reaction and to store the information as in a scrapbook to which I could later return if I wanted to relive the moment.

Secondly, the journal allowed me to pour out my struggles. I had to come to terms with the bureaucracy, the unnerving lack of information for Westerners unable to read Chinese, the sense of dependency as a foreigner, the complicated institutional power structure, and my inability at times to understand even my best friends. China was like a maze, and the writing helped me establish landmarks to find my way through it. It allowed me to process my impressions on paper, as if I were sharing with a patiently listening friend. By describing my confusion I sorted through it, ordered it, structured it, until I saw more clearly. Keeping a journal helped me retain a high level of curiosity about living in China. I felt I had only scratched the surface of what there was to know and that I needed to listen and learn more each day.

This book is an invitation for the reader to accompany me on a journey. How would *you* like to go to China? Come, let me show you the country and its people. I look forward to sharing with you the ups and downs of being a foreigner in China today. Most of all, I want you to meet my friends.

Ingrid Rogers
North Manchester, Indiana
June 1988

A daycare worker taking a group of children for a walk

Artist woodburning on plywood

*A fisherman
selling prawn*

*A blackboard in a
Chinese Middle School.
The girl pictured
prepared all of the
writing shown.*

A man in his garden

*The Protestant
Church of Dalian
with a membership
of 4000*

Ingrid, David, and Stefan Rogers with Chinese students in a typical dorm room

Angela Rogers with her classmates after school

1

The First Glimpse

Arrival

"Ken, are you awake?" I whispered, gently poking my husband.

"Now I am," he said drily.

"I can't get back to sleep. What time is it?"

"Only two a.m. One o'clock in the afternoon in Indiana. Just think, if we were home you would have slept through the whole morning."

"Very funny!"

"Sshhh! Talk more quietly, or you'll wake the children."

Angela and Stefan were asleep in the bunkbeds on the opposite wall. I listened to their steady breathing and felt a deep sense of relief to have them here with us. A six-months separation would have been unbearable. This way, we could live through the adventure together and, just in case the dream of China would turn into a nightmare, we would be there to comfort one another.

"Do you mind talking about what happened today?" I asked Ken who had continued dozing.

"Yesterday, you mean. No, I don't mind. Go ahead."

"I still can't believe we are in Beijing," I said. "Pinch me."

"Good enough?"

"Yeah."

Ken propped himself up, fully awake now. "You know what the most beautiful moment was for me so far?" he asked.

"Tell me."

"It happened while we were waiting to have our passport checked. Remember the guard who came over to us and struck up a conversation with Stefan?"

Of course I remembered him. We had just set foot on Chinese soil when a tall man in an olive green uniform walked up, smiled broadly at our son, and started to try out his broken English. He and his colleagues were obviously intrigued with the blond curly hair of our eight-year-old and particularly pleased to find him so willing to converse with them. For Ken, this incident was significant because it set the tone for our stay. People had seemed eager to communicate with us. They had made us feel welcome and shown from the beginning that they wanted to be friends.

Beyond the passport control, Mr. Li from the Dalian Foreign Language Institute had greeted us in fluent English. Dressed in dark corduroy pants and a tweed jacket, he looked like an American Chinese. I felt relieved that we now had an interpreter. Fewer and fewer signs carried the English translation along with the Chinese. Surrounded by a sea of unfamiliar sounds, Li's "Hello" sounded immensely comforting. After helping us store our luggage, he skillfully maneuvered our groups through the complicated Chinese system of "making arrangements." Back in Indiana I had assumed naively that we would be able to take care of this process ourselves. Based on previous experiences abroad, I had figured if no one were at the airport to greet us, we could simply find someone who spoke English, buy new flight tickets, and continue to Dalian. Things are not that simple in China. No tickets can be purchased directly at the airport. The right place is the ticket office in downtown Beijing. So having locked up our suitcases, we soon found ourselves on a rickety old bus bouncing toward the capital city.

The day before in Tokyo while enjoying the comfort and luxury of the Narita Hotel, we had begun to wonder whether most of our Asia experience would not be all that different from what we were used to back home in the United States. But this brief ride proved that, indeed, we had entered a different culture. Beyond the trees, on both sides of the road, were walled-in brick living quarters, clean but extremely crowded and without glassed windows. Sections of Beijing looked like slums except that the streets were immaculate and the people moved about in such a purposeful way. All were warmly clad; no one seemed malnourished or much richer or poorer than the rest. With excitement we took in the outside markets, the first pagoda-shaped roofs, the flood of bicycles moving artfully between buses, taxis, and pedestrians.

What was the trick to surviving in this traffic? It seemed unwise to stop or hesitate while crossing streets because pedestrians as well as cyclists and bus drivers calculated their speed on the premise that the same movement would continue. Once our bus swung around a terribly crowded intersection where a mob of people was gathered in one place.

"What's that over there?" I asked Li. "A demonstration of some sort?"

"I don't think so," he said. "It looks more like an accident."

Apparently, assumptions about the flow of traffic weren't always correct!

At the ticket office in Beijing we settled down to another lengthy period of waiting while Li made arrangements to book our flight. Every now and then I walked over to watch the process. Strangely enough, it wasn't simply a matter of walking up to the counter and buying a ticket. A long explanation of why and wherefore accompanied the transaction. Each little decision seemed to require the most detailed information, which the customers graciously volunteered. On the other side of each window were three to five preoccupied clerks, all very eager to help, busily shuffling papers and trying to understand what needed to be done. Upon hearing the request, they engaged in a lively debate of what might be the best next step. Unusual situations (and as foreigners we probably fell into that category) required that a "higher up" be consulted before the decision was made. Advice and recommendations were passed back and forth like ping-pong balls. I watched with fascination. The other people in line patiently endured the lengthy process. They simply crowded around the window to listen with interest to the debates.

Amazingly, it took Li less than an hour to reserve our flights to Dalian for the next day. He himself must have been surprised to see things work out this smoothly.

"What did you just sign there?" I ask him after he finished writing in a green book which the woman at the ticket counter had handed to him.

"I praised the woman for her service," said Li. "We don't tip in China. If we appreciate what officials have done, we can write a note in their book. Then their superiors will see that they have treated their customers well."

While we were waiting, Stefan had proceeded to make friends with the employees at a nearby candy store. He had such an easy time relating to strangers! Part of it is the attraction of his blond hair and blue eyes, but perhaps an even more helpful asset is his personality; he does not mind being stared at, and he loves to talk to people. By the end of this episode, the group of Chinese who had gathered around him in the candy story had figured out that he was eight years old, and the manager had given him a package of dried fish as a special treat.

When I tried to disengage him from the group, the adults were in the process of teaching him how to say his age in Chinese. We both repeated the words, but despite my careful pronunciation they did not seem satisfied with my performance and made us say it over and over again. Finally I realized that the first syllable was spoken on a higher level. Once again I repeated, and this time the whole group smiled and cheered.

We took a taxi to the Beijing Sports Institute, where we were supposed to spend the night before proceeding to Dalian the next morning. Li had reserved rooms in the regular student dorms. We were glad for the opportunity to experience normal Chinese housing rather than a fancy Western-type hotel. Actually, even this building with its spartan furnishings, cement floors, and bare walls was probably very luxurious compared to the regular living quarters of the average Chinese.

"Mom?" came a quiet sound from the upper bunk across the room.

"What, Angela?"

"What time is it?"

"Four a.m. Try to sleep some more."

"I need to use the bathroom."

"It's just down the hall, to your left."

Thirty seconds later she was back, a puzzled look in her eyes.

"Mom?"

"What's the matter?"

"There is no bathroom."

"Oh?"

"Come and see, please."

Angela took my hand and pulled me out the door. I already knew what was bothering her and could barely keep from chuckling.

"Look, there's no seat!"

Upon which I proceeded to teach my puzzled daughter the art of squatting over an Asian latrine.

It was useless to try to go back to sleep. We got dressed and took a walk around the college premises until daybreak. Li called us in for breakfast.

"Do you want Chinese or Western-style food?" he asked. We opted for "going native," eager to adjust to our new environment and curious about what the new dishes would taste like. Perhaps we should have chosen the Western breakfast just to see how close this version came to what we were used to eating back home. They served us a bland, unsweetened rice porridge, a bulging roll of steamed bread, and a dish of spicy seaweed and other strange vegetables dotted with boiled nuts.

"Do you want some sour milk with your meal?" asked Li.

"Sour milk? Ah—no, thanks. I don't believe so."

We wanted to be careful not to arrive at Dalian with our first intestinal infection. But Angela, who couldn't help trying a sip, discovered that we had passed up a delicious yogurt drink.

The plane for Dalian was scheduled to leave at noon, so we decided to spend the rest of the morning downtown near the Forbidden City. Very few foreigners were out sightseeing, perhaps because it was a weekday or because this is the off-season. We mingled freely with the crowd as American tourists among Chinese tourists. Many stared at us, but since everything about China was still so new, I am sure we must have stared back just as intently. Stefan with his blond locks attracted the most attention. When we lined up at the foot of a golden lion to let Li take a photograph, many other Chinese stopped and took our picture as well.

One should schedule at least a day for the Forbidden City. Unfortunately Li soon reminded us that we had to get to the airport. Perhaps there would be time, later in the year, to return to Beijing. Before we knew it we found ourselves on the plane to Dalian. For some reason the plane was only half filled; but, curiously, all the passengers were crowded into the front half of the seating area. On an American flight passengers would have been spread out, but apparently the Chinese either like to be close together or the ticket office has to assign seats in order until the whole plane is filled.

The dean and two other officials from the Dalian Foreign Language Institute awaited us at the airport. They had come in a big bus, expecting that a group of Americans would bring plenty of luggage. After the introductions and our expression of thanks for Li's competent handling of the trip, we mounted the bus for the last stretch of our journey.

Our New Home

"This is your apartment," said Li. We stopped to catch our breath, having climbed to the fifth floor of what they call the "Foreign Experts Building." The door opened to a room-size hallway that stood empty except for a small refrigerator in one corner. To the left, a set of swinging glass doors led to the living room furnished with a cupboard, a desk, two red folding chairs, and a stuffed armchair draped with white covers and a yellowish towel. A thin, bright red carpet added a cheerful color and contrasted prettily with the plain white wallpaper and beige curtains.

Housemaster Wang, who had helped carry up suitcases, eagerly watched for the reaction on our faces. He pointed to the television on top of the cupboard, turned it on, and looked at us as if expecting us to break out in delight. We gave him a grateful smile. Realizing that we wouldn't understand Chinese, he made a series of grunting sounds and hand signs, deaf-mute fashion, as he explained how to work the machine. Li, who second-guessed that Americans probably knew how to adjust a television set, quickly translated the grunts into English.

The children proceeded to claim the adjacent room as theirs and explored its two twin beds, another desk, a large built-in closet, and a narrow balcony facing south. The bedroom left for Ken and me was slightly smaller, with a large window to the north from which we could see clear across town as far as the harbor and beyond to a narrow strip of land at the horizon across the bay.

Our hosts had obviously done their best to make us comfortable. The apartment was full of luxury items most Chinese only dream of: refrigerator, color television, a bathtub, even a washing machine. The kitchen was tiny and poorly designed, with a huge tiled sink on the one side, a tiled work area with one gas burner on the other, and a hanging cupboard fastened so high that I could not reach the upper shelves; but I was not expecting to cook much anyway. Meals for the foreign faculty, we were told, would be served downstairs three times a day.

"Is everything to your liking?" asked Vice President Sheng who had come to welcome us.

"Oh, definitely," Ken reassured him. He had just finished looking down from our balcony onto a row of tiny shacks inhabited by local Chinese families. How many rooms did they have? Perhaps one, or at most two. How would they feel if they saw our luxurious quarters?

"We know this is not as comfortable as your home in America," said Mr. Sheng as if in answer to my question. "We do the best we can, but of course this is not very nice. We hope you will excuse us. . . .

"Oh, this is beautiful," I hastened to contradict. "It's large and light and cozy!"

Pleased, Mr. Sheng nodded his head, smiled, and shook hands with us. Welcome to our Institute."

"Do you want to take a nap or go eat supper?" I asked Ken after we had finished storing the empty suitcases on the upper shelf of the children's closet. "We'd better eat while we can," he said. Considering our bare kitchen shelves, we hardly had a choice. Besides, curiosity won over fatigue.

The restaurant on the ground floor was spacious and well lit, with brightly colored tablecloths, red thermoses, porcelain rice bowls, and chopsticks on each of five round tables.

"Hi! My name is Alicia," said a small woman of about forty-five. "And this is Claudine and her husband Jacques. Claudine teaches French. They are from Canada."

After introducing ourselves, we joined Alicia and the younger couple at their table.

"Will you be teaching English here, or are you just passing through?" Claudine asked.

"We'll be here for six months," said Ken. "We are starting an exchange program with the Dalian Institute. Teachers from this school get to spend time at our colleges, and our students come here to learn Chinese and teach English."

"Do you already know Chinese?"

"I wish! No, we'll all start together from scratch next week."

"You are really fortunate," said Alicia. "We have been here since last fall, and the teaching load is so heavy that we don't have time to study Chinese. I can read a few characters, but not nearly enough to read the street signs. Claire and Simon Hopkins are the only American teachers who can begin to carry on a simple conversation in Chinese."

"Where are they?"

"Who, Claire and Simon? They are still on winter break. Ella Brown and Susan McLean are still out, too. We just came back from a trip ourselves the day before yesterday. This is the time in between semesters."

"Did you travel on your own?"

"Yes, we went to Harbin, which is over a day's journey north of here, to see the ice sculptures. You really ought to go visit Harbin yourselves. Try to get away before classes start. You would not believe how marvelously intricate those sculptures are. Palaces, fountains, statues, flowers—all made of ice!"

I was about to say that, as much as her description intrigued me, I couldn't possibly see leaving Dalian since it would take us at least a week to get settled. Just then a teenage girl with a pretty round face and prominent check bones carried in our supper. *"Ni hao* (hello)," we greeted her with the only Chinese words we had mastered so far. *"Ni hao,"* she responded with a giggle.

"This is Jing," explained Alicia. "She is very sweet. In her spare time she studies English so she can explain to us foreigners what food we are going to have. We have already taught her the names of the basic dishes. Claire and Jing tutor each other."

Jing brought us each a bowl of rice, tomato soup, and delicious strips of breaded pork. Alicia, Claudine, and Jacques deftly helped themselves with their chopsticks. It took us a little longer to get hold of the food, but we managed. Between bites, we bombarded our new colleagues with questions. "Who else lives in this place?" "Are there any children?" "What nationalities are represented?"

Patiently they took turns filling us in. "There are seven Americans besides you: the three of us, Claire and Simon from Arkansas, Ella from Tennessee, and Susan from Wisconsin. The largest group of teachers is from Japan. They eat down here too, but they have a different arrangement for their meals and usually sit by themselves. A Japanese family with two children lives just two stories below you. No, sorry, there are no Germans. No Russians either."

"But they told us German and Russian were offered at the school," I objected, disappointed.

"Well," said Jacques with slight sarcasm, "in China they sometimes talk like a situation is real when in fact it's still in the planning stage."

We launched into questions about the neighborhood. "Where do you shop?" "How do you get downtown?" "Where is the nearest post office?"

Amused about our curiosity, Claudine laughed out loud. "Take your time! You'll soon get a chance to find out all about it. If you like, we can go for a walk together tomorrow."

"I remember how curious I was when I first came last fall," said Alicia. "I had the same kind of enthusiasm. Only there was no one to help me until Claire and Simon got back from their summer trip."

"What happened to your enthusiasm?" I asked.

"Oh, she still has it," interrupted Claudine. "More than the rest of us, anyway. Alicia always puts up with whatever comes. So now she's gotten stuck with more teaching hours than anyone else. You have to put your foot down, or they'll exploit you. Being here gets old after a while. But you'll learn soon enough!"

I suddenly felt uneasy. It was nice to be initiated by experienced folk, but I wanted to acquaint myself with the culture open-mindedly and at my own speed. Why were Claudine and Jacques so cynical about China? Perhaps they had a reason to be, but I wasn't ready to hear about it at this point. I wanted to find out for myself, and I felt I deserved time just to enjoy and delight in what I would see.

Fortunately the conversation shifted again. We soon left, too tired to absorb even one more bit of information.

A Walk Through the Neighborhood

A day later Alicia knocked at our door with a shopping bag in hand.

"I need to go downtown. Do you want to come along?"

"Sure. Can the children come, too?"

"Yes, I don't mind. I'll see you at the front door in about five minutes, all right?"

When we joined her, Alicia was skimming through a letter that had been posted for her in the window of the doorkeeper's room.

"This is where you pick up your mail," she said. "Of course it will be awhile until your first letters come."

"How long does it take usually?"

"Oh, about ten to twelve days, I would say. Sometimes overseas mail ends up in the English Department and has to be rerouted to our building; then it takes even longer."

"Why do we need a doorkeeper?"

"Good question," Alicia said with a grin as she headed out the door. "Most public buildings have one here. They say it's for security, but Dalian is a very safe place. Maybe it's a way to provide jobs. Claudine and Claire are convinced it's to keep track of which Chinese students have contacts with foreigners. Who knows?"

I pondered all these possibilities as we trudged downhill through remnants of last week's snow that had turned into slush.

"The building right there ahead of us with the gaudy posters is a movie theater. Catty-corner across from it is the closest grocery store."

"Look, Mom, there's Superman!" Stefan shouted excitedly. Sure enough, the painting above the theater entrance showed his hero, larger than life-size, flying proudly through the sky in a cloak embellished with Chinese characters. I looked for the grocery store on the other side but could not see any.

"Most indoor stores are sort of hidden away," Alicia filled us in. "They look like normal houses, and there is hardly any advertising. The local people just know where the stores are. Do you want to look inside?"

She led us up a few stairs and through a doorway blocked by a heavy curtain to keep the cold out. On the right, glassed-in, was the meat counter with a few bony or fatty cuts that didn't look too appetizing. The shelves straight ahead were filled with liquor and spices. Aside from the batches of cookies on the counter top, nothing tempted me to spend money.

"You will need ration cards for the cookies," said Alicia who had followed my eyes.

"And what are those?"

"Here, I'll show you." She pulled out a stack of colorful tiny bills with numbers at the corner. "Li can give you a supply. I seldom know what kind of card they want, so I just hold them all up and let them pick out the right one. Apparently you need them to buy rice and other grain products. Some things that are rationed you can get without the cards simply by paying a little more, but others you can't. It's rather confusing."

We continued our walk on down the hill another block, past a small park on the right, until we got to the bus stop.

"That green container on the post over there is the nearest mail box. Now, if you want to walk downtown, just keep going straight for another fifteen minutes and you'll end up in Zhong Shan Square, with the Bank of China right on the square and the main shopping area only a block further north."

"Let's take the bus, Mom," the children begged. For them it was an adventure. Coming from a small town, they weren't used to riding buses.

"You may not enjoy it," warned Alicia. "The buses tend to be terribly crowded."

Sure enough, about twenty people were already waiting at the stop.

"Hadn't we better wait for the next one?" I suggested. "How often do the buses run?"

"They come about every five minutes; but waiting doesn't help because the next one will be just as full. The only way to get on is to keep pushing. I hate it. Sometimes I think the Chinese make a sport out of trying to squeeze 150 people into a bus that can hold forty. Watch out, here it comes. Are you ready?"

I stepped back to watch the scene. As soon as the bus stopped, a cluster formed around the door, leaving a narrow path for those wanting off. Gradually, persistently, fifteen passengers forced their way out. As soon as the last one had made it through, the lump of those waiting tightened. Slowly, with steady pressure and some shoving, they worked themselves in one by one. "Come on," Alicia yelled, "there's room!"

Room? Where? She must be kidding. But Angela and Stefan had already joined the battle, so I could not stay back. I set my foot on the stairs and felt the doors reluctantly close behind me. The kids alternated laughs with little shrieks of panic. A step at a time, we maneuvered ourselves into the middle of the aisle to find some breathing space. "I'll pay for you," Alicia volunteered and held up the change. Some other passenger picked it up and handed it to the attendent near the door. The change and four tickets came back the same way.

"How can they keep track of who has paid and who hasn't?

"I have no idea, but they seem to manage. I have seen them prevent people without a ticket from getting off."

We stopped with a jolt. I reached for the iron bar overhead to avoid stepping on another person's foot or crushing the passenger in front of me. As tightly packed as the bus was, at least we didn't have to worry about falling over.

"Did you pay attention to the stops?" asked Alicia. "Sorry you can't see much. The third stop is across from the Friendship Store, where you can buy souvenirs with foreign exchange currency. It's near the harbor and the Seamen's Club. I get off there every now and then to buy Western bread in a little bakery next to the Seamen's Club. If you like, I'll show it to you sometime."

"How much longer till we get downtown?"

"Two more stops—five altogether. You sound ready to get out of here!"

I grinned, admitting she was right. When we finally arrived I pressed forward, grateful for the broad-shouldered man in front of me who broke through the crowd like a wedge. A few more steps through another cluster of people and we were back in the open air, laughing, panting, breathing a sigh of relief.

"I can see why you prefer walking!"

"It isn't always bad," Alicia reassured me. "We must have hit the rush hour. But you are right, it's almost as fast on foot and a whole lot more comfortable."

I was surprised to see so many people in the streets on a week-day morning. What were they all up to? Why weren't they at work? Didn't China claim to have full employment?

"One of my students told me that the work units give people different days off," said Alicia. "In a city of two million, like Dalian, that means perhaps 100,000 employees are not at work on any given day, and many of them use the opportunity to shop. Look, here is the outdoor market. Tienjin Street has no through traffic, only booths on both sidewalks. You can find almost anything from dishes to tennis shoes and padded underwear."

We took a leisurely stroll through the crowds. Every now and then a mother called her child's attention to us: *"Wai guo ren!"* The child gave us a questioning, curious glance. Foreigners. How strange to be so obviously different! For the first time in my life I was a racial minority, needing to accept that anywhere in town, no matter how dense the crowd, I would stand out like a torch.

Alicia didn't seem to mind the attention and began bargaining for a pretty woolen jacket. I envied her language skills. Although she didn't speak full sentences, she at least could make herself understood and find out the prices.

"I feel helpless and stupid not knowning any Chinese," I confessed.

"Oh, don't worry. You'll learn the basic phrases soon. By the way, did you notice the hand motions that salesman made? The Chinese have a way of signalling numbers one through ten on one hand."

She showed us the motions and said the numbers in Chinese. Angela and Stefan quickly learned how to sign, but none of us retained the words. Chinese syllables ran through my brain like water through a sieve; I could not recall them.

"Let's go home," Alicia said after we had browsed for an hour in Dalian's biggest department store. This time we walked all the way, past Zhong Shan Square and up the hill back to the Institute. I was grateful for my comfortable winter boots as I anticipated how much walking we would do over the coming months.

A Technological Marvel

Our computer is working! It may seem silly to be so jubilant about a functioning word processor, but for me that little machine makes all the difference. Now I can write about all that has happened so far without having to trust my forgetful brain; I can pour out my frustrations without having to bore anyone else; and I can share my impressions with folks back in Indiana simply by reprinting excerpts from my journal.

Buying the portable computer had been a gamble. We were not sure of the electrical current and feared that frequent power failures would wipe out files. As a precaution Ken had bought a model which ran on rechargeable batteries, along with several step-down transformers to tackle the problem with the current. The word processor is running on electrical power right now, but as soon as the power gets cut off, the batteries will take over automatically. We will keep a desk lamp burning whenever we run the computer, so that we will notice a power failure right away and can save what we have written before the battery runs down.

In our primitive surroundings, the fancy equipment looks bizarre. We lack basic supplies like pots and pans, a coat rack, or even a clothesline. Hot water is available only in the middle of the day after everyone else is finished taking showers, and the heat is turned off between ten in the morning and five in the afternoon—but there, on our desk, sits a technological wonder which has managed so far to overcome the complexities of life in China.

The machine works smoothly, as if being transplanted into a different world did not matter in the least. If only the adjustment were as easy for the rest of us! It will help me to have the computer because writing is a security blanket for me, a way to impose structure on a confusing environment. Whatever it is that puzzles me, once I have named it, put it into words, it no longer dominates me. I have shaped it into something I can recognize and identify.

A Community of Foreigners

I have not yet introduced our four Brethren Colleges Abroad students. All four have courageously thrown themselves into life in China. Unlike new students at United States campuses, they have received no orientation by the administrators of the Foreign Language Institute, but it doesn't seem to trouble them. They are finding their way around with remarkable ease. At mealtime we hear about their latest escapades. It is fun to observe their eagerness to make this place their home for the next six months. All four students look attractive by Western standards. Peggy with her reddish-blond locks and bright blue eyes is sensational. In a Chinese crowd, she'll be as easy to find as a yellow plate on a brown tablecloth. Lisa with her dark hair and sparkling hazel eyes is equally Western because of the way she dresses. A little plump, she covers up her weight problem with fashionable, attractive clothing. Bob is six feet tall and like Stefan and Peggy has blue eyes and curly blond hair. He is a sanguine type of person, bright, perceptive, easily smiling. Craig with his straight, black hair probably has the best chance of passing unnoticed in a Chinese crowd. More quiet then Bob and a little shy, he might go undetected among Americans as well. But he is friendly and polite. His Southern way of addressing us as "Ma'am" and "Sir" has a strange ring to it that will take some time getting used to. Perhaps I can talk him into using first names, which Bob has already started doing.

"Did you find enough room to store all your outfits?" Bob teased Lisa at dinner time. He and Craig had brought two suitcases each, whereas Lisa had come with seven.

Just then Jing entered with a new set of dishes. The food has been excellent so far. Alicia tells us that fish is the most expensive protein food around here, and yet it is served to us frequently. Every day new exotic spicy tidbits of crunchy vegetables show up in our diet. And yet some of it, to the surprise of our cooks, does not make our mouths water the way it would a Chinese person's. Today we were surprised with black seaweed soup and a plate full of squid. Except for Bob, we all decided to stick with the bowl of rice that always accompanies the meal. Jing and the second waitress, who speaks not a word of English, were very concerned about our lack of enthusiasm. They rushed in with note pads and pencil to ask Claire what kind of dishes we like.

"Isn't it amazing how they go out of their way to please us?" Peggy said, astonished.

"You just wait." Claudine had to put a damper on her enthusiasm. "The food won't stay that good. It's been much better since your group got here, but it won't last."

"They really do try to cook what we like," Claire contradicted her. "If you don't care for this," Simon joined in, "you should try the food in the student cafeteria!"

"Yes, but we also pay three times as much."

To avoid any more trivial bickering, Claire switched to dietary tales of woe from her recent trip to Southern China. Somewhere along the way she had eaten spoiled food which not only gave her terrible bouts of diarrhea but also made her face and arms swell up like balloons.

"You should have seen her!" Simon rolled his eyes, pretending despair. "For a whole week she looked like this."

Everyone, including Claire, burst out laughing at his mimicry.

15

Now that all the foreign teachers are back, a sense of camaraderie is developing among some of us. I feel especially attracted to Claire who has a gentleness and charm that makes everyone want to be her friend. Soon after her return from winter break she invited me down to her apartment just a floor below ours. What a beautiful, homey place it is! She and Simon have managed to pick up some wicker furniture in the South of China. Throw carpets, paintings, plants, a bed turned into a sofa with the help of a handmade spread and stuffed cushions, glass cabinets full of dishes, and dozens of little items that are not normally available in stores make this apartment unique. More surprisingly still, it has become a retreat for Chinese students and English-speaking Chinese who are not part of our Institute. Claire and Simon have an open-door policy that is real, unforced, irresistible. The whole place breathes hospitality and simple comfort.

I admire their goldfish which lazily swims in a glass bowl on Simon's desk.

"Would Angela and Stefan like a fish?" Simon asks, lighting his pipe. "I can get them one downtown."

"They'd love it! Would you?"

"Sure. No problem."

"By the way," adds Claire, "could we borrow your kids every now and then? I love children. It would be fun to take them for a ride on the Ferris wheel at Labor Park. Do you mind?"

"Not at all!" Do I mind? Does any mother mind getting a little break every now and then? It will be wonderful for Angela and Stefan to have adult friends who enjoy spending time with them.

"I had a baby once," Claire says quietly. "It was stillborn. My boy would have been eighteen this year."

I look at her in silent empathy, then give her a hug. How easy it is to take children for granted. "I'll be glad to lend you mine, whenever you feel like having them around."

Learning Chinese

"Have you had any classes yet?" asks Claudine, the French teacher from Quebec.

"We had our first three hours of Chinese this morning. The English conversation classes won't start till the end of the week."

16

"What was the Chinese class like?"

"Well . . ." Lisa pauses, then starts giggling.

"I can't tell whether we are going too fast or too slowly," says Craig, stabbing his omelette with his chopsticks to separate a piece he can pick up. "A lot of *a*'s, *e*'s, and *u*'s, if you know what I mean."

Impressions from class flashed back to mind. In front, behind a small wooden podium, stands teacher He (not pronounced like the English *he,* but more like a throaty German ch sound followed by the indefinite article *a).* Li is with us for the first hour to help with introductions and explanations. The chair of the Chinese department comes to welcome us with a polite little speech that we have come to recognize as customary. Ken delivers the equally predictable rejoinder on behalf of our Brethren Colleges Abroad group. Both parties look forward to a successful six months of cooperation and mutual benefit. In the coming weeks I am sure Ken will grow more and more comfortable with the skill of saying nothing at all in these gentle exchanges; it is the gesture that matters, not the content.

Teacher He speaks no English. Once the guests leave, we are on our own without an interpreter and with textbooks made in China for foreign students. Under each line of Chinese, the characters are first transcribed into the phonetic pinyin, then translated into English and French. Teacher He does remarkably well with the little he has to work with. He gets us to repeat, time and again, until the pronunciation seems satisfactory and he can reward us with a broad smile and nod. If we don't manage, the smile is still there, but the nod is replaced with a troubled look of concern in his gentle eyes.

"Zenmeyang a?" he says, exaggerating the tones like a melody.

"Zenmeyang a?" Craig repeats, ignoring the pitches. Teacher He tries again. Same response. Third try, his eyes looking sadder. Still Craig doesn't catch on.

"Watch the tones. Down on the last syllable," I whisper to Craig, who is about to despair. In the next round, he does better. Relieved, if not quite satisfied, teacher He moves on to Peggy. We all take a turn. Then he introduces a section without the pinyin transcription. He wants us to read the Chinese characters. After all, we have practiced these sentences for the past hour.

The trouble is that none of us has paid the least bit of attention to the characters. We all focused on the pinyin, relying on the accent marks to help us with the tones. How are we to know what these characters mean? Quickly, we leaf through the last pages to hunt for clues. This must be some sort of substitution drill: you are doing fine; the teacher is doing fine; the students are doing fine (ha!). After ten minutes of puzzled looks and frustration, He tables the exercise and moves on to polish our accents. The vowels come out okay, but some of the consonants are hard to tell apart. *Ji, gi, xi,* we practice patiently. *Za, ca, sa, zha, cha, sha.* One by one, we can repeat them to He's satisfaction, but as part of sentences they become blurred. Everyone, including He, breathes a sigh of relief when the hour is up.

"Do you remember any of the characters?" Bob asks at lunch time.

"Are you kidding? I wish we could just stick with the pinyin and not bother learning the written language." Lisa wrinkles her nose at the tomato soup and pushes it over to Craig. "Want a second helping?"

"Yeah, I'm hungry enough."

"It won't work," Claire continues the discussion about Chinese. "You'll need the writing in the long run. And if you stick with it, it'll get to be fun. I love drawing characters."

"Hmm." Peggy gives her a doubtful look.

"You know, there is one character I remember," says Ken. "The one for student. It has three short dots on top that look like a butch haircut."

Claire laughs. "Not to disappoint you, but I think you'll find plenty more butch haircuts once you are past your first fifty characters!"

Anyway, it's a start. And mastering fifty characters seems a long way in the future.

Teaching English

Teaching their first English conversation classes was a big event for our BCA students. We invited them to come over after their lesson to share and unwind. Craig and Bob arrived first.

"How did it go?" With my own classes still ahead, I was especially curious to hear the news.

"I spent the hour with introductions and then told them a bit about myself," said Bob. "It went pretty well, but I wish they had been more ready to speak. I wanted to ask questions or to suggest topics of interest, but no one responded. It seems like they just sit and wait for the teacher to tell them what to do. The whole class was left up to me. I never expected I'd have to talk so much!"

"My class was like that too," Craig agreed. "I ran out of things to say. I wanted them just to discuss freely, but no one said a word. I wonder what it is in the Chinese education system that makes them so reluctant to take the initiative."

"Maybe they just aren't used to that kind of teaching," I ventured. "It could be that their teachers all lecture rather than encourage dialogue."

"But how can they learn conversational English if they refuse to talk?" Craig sounded frustrated. "And another thing that bothers me is that the students make fun of a classmate who gives a wrong answer. I finally got someone to volunteer a few sentences, and then everyone giggled. That would make me give up trying too!"

I was surprised. "How did the student seem to feel about it?"

"Oh, not too badly. He grinned and apologized for doing a poor job. I was glad that at least someone had spoken up."

I tried to think of other reasons why the Chinese students might be so reluctant. Maybe they didn't want to ask questions because they were afraid to offend. Or perhaps it takes a while to warm up to a new acquaintance and they will get more talkative with greater familiarity. It could also be that they are not used to teachers so close to their own age. I can hardly wait to begin my own classes. Right now we are just observing behavior patterns without having the slightest clue what makes a person act a certain way. We will have to be careful not to jump to quick conclusions about Chinese students because of these first impressions. Claudine made another critical comment at supper yesterday. "Their language skills are not that great," she said. "Most of the students can impress you with a repertoire of set phrases or little speeches they have memorized, like 'I live in Dalian. Dalian is famous for its many kinds of apples.' Or, 'We are very happy that you are our teacher. We need much help with our pronunciation. We look forward to learning from you.' They will reiterate these sentences over and over again, with excellent intonation and precision, like little automatons."

I found myself resenting Claudine's judgment but unable to counter it. Claire later filled me in that Claudine is tired of being in China. She is counting the days until she gets to go back to Canada, only the contract is holding her here. Her resentment comes through in the many negative comments she makes at mealtime. I am determined not to let her influence my image of the student body. Surely those at our Language Institute are very bright. It is an elite school; only the best get to come. Memorization of phrases seems dull to us, but perhaps for language acquisition the method isn't bad. Now that I am learning Chinese characters I wish I were more skilled at memorization myself!

Lisa joined us forty-five minutes later than we had expected.

"What took you so long?" Craig grinned at her while she was catching her breath.

"My, it takes energy to get up here on fifth floor," she said, panting. "You wouldn't believe what just happened to me."

"Tell us!"

"Well, I got through the class all right, but when the hour was over, no one got up to leave. So I kept talking some more. I tried to hint repeatedly that the students could leave now, but all stuck to their seats like they were glued to them. This went on for almost an hour. Boy, did I ever feel awkward! I finally picked up my coat and left."

"Sounds like the German schools," I said. The teachers come and go, but the students stay put."

"Why didn't anybody tell me?"

"I heard about it from Alicia," said Bob, helping himself to another cookie. "The whole student body is divided into groups of twenty to twenty-five, each of which have a room that is 'theirs.' When they don't have class, they use the room to study."

"You mean to say I should have left an hour ago, and the students were just too polite to point it out to me?"

"I'm afraid so. Here, have a cookie and take it easy." Bob handed her the tray and a cup of tea. "Now we'll know better next time."

I told the group about my first day in high school as a German exchange student, when I had the reverse but equally embarrassing experience. The principal had taken me to my first class, but as soon as the bell rang, all the students jumped out of their seats and stormed out the door as if a fire alarm had gone off. I stood there dumfounded, not knowing what to do, until the teacher finally explained that I had to find my way to a new room.

I guess we all operate out of our preconceived notions of what is "normal." Very little is normal here.

My First Conversation Class

"Can you stay and talk some more?" asks Song Zhihui after the lesson has ended.

"Sure, but let's go out in the hallway so the others can continue their studies." I remember Lisa's experience well. Having had advanced warning, it is easy to pick up clues that the students virtually live in their classrooms during the day. More books than one could carry are neatly stacked at the front of their small desks; personal items such as letters and photographs are left in the storage area below; and no bell rings to signal the end of a lesson.

The group I just taught is called the "Finance Class." They are older students, mostly in their late twenties and thirties.

"Why did you get such a strange title for your class?" I ask Song.

"Because most of my classmates are tax collectors or accountants."

"But you aren't?"

"No, I'm a teacher. I teach English in Tienjin, and my work unit wants me to get more skilled in the language. I was very fortunate to be selected to come here."

"Are all your classmates sent by their work units?"

"Sure. We couldn't afford to pay for it ourselves."

"Why are you going back at this time in your life?"

"Most of us missed out on a good education during our teenage years because of the Cultural Revolution. We were sent to the countryside. We didn't get to study math or literature or foreign languages. Now that times have changed, some of us are getting a chance to make up. I am really happy to come here. Unfortunately, my English is very bad."

I have come to recognize this last sentence as a polite phrase, used even by students whose English skills are exceptional. Song Zhihui is certainly doing very well. Her sentences don't come out

21

with native fluency, but she has no trouble expressing what she wants to say. I assure her I am impressed with her language ability.

"You flatter me," she says with a wink. "That's an expression we just learned in Miss Alicia's class." Song has a broad smile that brings a dimple to her cheek.

By now we are surrounded by a group of four or five other students who hope to catch segments of our conversation. They begin to ask questions about our family: why we have come, how old our children are, how much Chinese we already know. I answer patiently, regretting somewhat that the opportunity to get better acquainted with Song has to be tabled. Where does one go for privacy around here? With eight people per dorm room and twenty-five in a class, it is hard to find a vacant spot for a quiet conversation. Maybe once it gets warmer we can go for walks together.

On my way back to the apartment I relive the lesson of the past hour. Like Bob and Craig, I spent most of the time with introductions; but unlike their students, mine don't have English names. In a way I am relieved. This older group would rather be Zhang Xiaoxi, Gu Chenyang, and Zhao Aiguo than Betty, Roger, or Tim. Who can blame them? There is something distasteful about imposing a new name on a Chinese person who already has been named in a much more appropriate fashion.

The students took turns presenting themselves. First the class monitor:

"I am Wang Yang. It means 'deep ocean.' I am from Sechuan province."

"Wang Yang," I repeat. Someone giggles. I probably didn't get the tones properly and turned the deep ocean into something funny.

"My name is Li Meiling," says the woman in the blue sweater at the next desk. "Meiling means 'beautiful and clever.' "

"I am Wei Heping, and my first name means 'peace.' Wei is a personal name, but it has the sound of words which mean either 'defend' or 'for.' "

I decide to write the names and their translations on a sheet of paper to help me remember.

"And what does your name mean?" the students ask me after I have jotted down all the Chinese words and their explanations. I look at them in surprise. No one has ever asked me that before.

"Nothing. It doesn't have a meaning." How embarrassing! It feels like deprivation. "Sometimes in the West we name our children after somebody we admire, but in my case I think my parents just liked the sound."

I wonder what words my parents would have chosen to describe me or to express their hopes and dreams for me when I was born. What name would I have liked? In Chinese, my married name comes out sounding like *Luo je se*—who knows what it means! Teacher He calls me "Lina" because my middle name is easier to pronounce than "Ingrid." Again I wonder what the Chinese syllables *Li-na* stand for. I'm almost afraid to ask.

It will take me a while to memorize these names, but I am determined to try. Knowing a person's name has to be the first step toward making friends. And I do want to get to know them better. They seemed a bit sceptical when they heard our group was trying to learn Chinese. They think it cannot be done, at least not in twenty-five weeks. Yet to try means showing good will and readiness to learn from them.

In all likelihood these students will be the key to Chinese society for me. The thousands of pedestrians I brush shoulders with in the streets are not really accessible. We can smile at each other, but we cannot communicate. This group, however, knows English. Better yet, they are immensely motivated to learn and to have contacts with native speakers. Until now Li, who had picked us up at the airport, was the only Chinese I could talk to; but for him being with foreigners is a job he often doesn't seem to like too well. In contrast, the students hunger for opportunities to speak with us. After class, many invited me to come back to talk as often as I want. Now I have a place to go with my curiosity about China. With as many questions as I have and with their eagerness to hear about the United States, I doubt that we'll ever run out of subjects to discuss.

Downtown with Alicia

I enjoy going shopping with Alicia. Not only does she know her way about, she also has a keen nose for bargains and will not be trapped into purchases she cannot afford.

"Do you want to go to the free market with me?" she called me on the telephone yesterday. "I need to get some eggs and nuts."

"Free as in 'out-of-doors,' or free as in 'take-what-you-like-without-paying'?"

Alicia laughed. "Free as in 'name your own price.' The merchants bring in the goods they have raised and sell them for whatever they think they can get. Sometimes the prices are higher, but sometimes lower than at the state market. If you are lucky, you find better quality produce."

"All right, I'll come along. Maybe I'll find some plates and a pot to cook with."

"Not at the free market. But if you like I can take you to a store on our way back."

Angela, Stefan, and I rushed to get our boots on, grabbed our winter coats, and ran downstairs where we found Alicia already waiting.

"This way." We crossed the soccer field and made our way downhill past the English and Japanese departments. "I hate going down that steep slope, but it's a nice short cut."

Stefan loved it. The air this past week had been crisp and dry, leaving the once muddy slope in solid but dusty condition. Stefan ran downhill, kicking up the dust with his heels until we were enveloped in a cloud of dirt.

"Sorry," I murmured apologetically on behalf of my son who was screeching with delight. A group of students looked at him, grinned, and reached to stroke his curly head.

Alicia shrugged her shoulders. "It doesn't matter. It's impossible to stay clean here anyway. See my socks?" she said, pulling up the leg of her pants. "They were white when I put them on this morning. Two hours in this polluted air, and they turn brownish grey around my ankles."

"The dust is pretty bad," I admitted. "Ken has caught some kind of throat infection from it. He's been coughing almost since we came here."

"I have it too," Alicia said, clearing her throat as if to prove it. "They burn so much coal in Dalian. It's supposed to be even worse in other cities, though, especially in Anshan and Shenyang to the north. That's the center of the steel industry. They tell me you can hardly breathe in those cities. Oh, see that woman on the bike over there?"

"The one with the nylon scarf clear over her face?"

"Yes. They wear it that way to keep from breathing in the dust particles. Up in Shenyang most cyclists cover their faces like that.

Fortunately in Dalian the air clears in the summer. And since we are surrounded by water on three sides, we always get a fresh breeze from the ocean."

"Do quite a few people get lung cancer, then?"

"I wouldn't be surprised. Plus a lot of the men smoke. The only good thing is that they walk a lot. They get more exercise. It probably keeps their hearts in shape."

"I haven't seen obese people."

"Oh, there are hardly any. Wait till summer, when all the padded underwear is stored away. Right now, they wear so many layers of clothing that some look fairly stout; but then you'll realize how thin they are."

"Maybe that's why everyone stared at my legs the day we arrived in Beijing!"

"What?"

"Oh, I just remembered that as we were sightseeing near the Forbidden City, people would point to my legs and talk to each other as if they couldn't believe their eyes. I thought there was something wrong with my boots. But they were probably just astounded that I would wear a skirt and nylons in the middle of winter."

"That's right. Have you seen anyone else in a dress? I would guess they felt very sorry for you!"

When we came past the small post office, I stopped to get some stamps. I had an envelope with me and pointed to what I wanted. The workers remembered the children from our last visit. They started chatting and laughing. The older woman, who had been especially friendly last time, pulled out a little black notebook with beautiful special stamps. One set showed panda bears, another scenes from the Forbidden City. Gratefully I purchased twice the number I had intended.

After a ten-minute walk we reached the "Free Market" where merchants behind three long rows of tables shouted to attract buyers pressing through the narrow aisles between rows. Primitive plastic roofing gave shelter against wind and precipitation. Angela and Stefan eyed the food with curiosity. Very little looked familiar: roots, fungus, seaweed, shells, a variety of fish and greenery I had never used in my cooking back home. Angela found some skinny chickens with their heads still attached while Stefan stared at a basket full of eels he mistook for snakes. I had expected more colorful displays and was disappointed with the drab, bleak, dirty heaps of food. What about carrots, celery, cauliflower, apples, and other fresh fruit?

"Meiyou," said Alicia. I already knew what that meant: Don't have. Sorry. Out of season.

We did find eggs, however. "It's a little risky to buy them," Alice pointed out. "The Chinese have a way of testing how fresh they are, but I haven't discovered how."

"Did you bring a container to carry them home in?"

"Just a little dish inside my bag. See how the Chinese do? They just put them loosely in a net."

"Won't they get squished that way?"

"You'd think, especially in the buses."

"Mom, come over here." Angela had discovered the peanuts. They were the unroasted kind, but Alicia assured us they were edible. "Put them in boiled water to get the skin off," she said. "They make a nice snack once you get used to the unsalted flavor."

I bought a pound, then followed Alicia into the state market to look for raisins. They had a few tiny, shrivelled-looking apples here and brownish bananas only slightly larger than my index finger. A little further down we found oranges, but they looked so overripe and battered that I hesitated. The atmosphere at the state market did not encourage me. Outside, the merchants approached the customers, praising and offering their produce. Here the salesmen and women were state employees who couldn't have cared less whether the food sold or not.

"Let's go to the department store," I suggested after we had found the raisins. I wanted at least one pan to cook in, for times when classes or other circumstances would keep me from getting back to our building for lunch or dinner. We found a nice aluminum one that I hoped would fit on our gas burner. I also picked up four little plates and a fancy pitcher for Ken to make iced tea.

"Where do you suppose one can get sugar?" I asked Alicia.

"Over there at the counter with all the candy, I suppose."

"How do you say *sugar* in Chinese?"

"No idea. Wait. I think it's something like *tang.* Try it."

I tried. The saleslady looked at me like I was a lunatic. *"Tang,"* I said again, trying each of the four tones. She held up a handful of candy, but when I turned it down, she shook her head and called a colleague. Who knows what I was saying!

26

"This is stupid," I told myself, feeling like a three-year-old. The colleague looked at me curiously. Once again I gave myself a push, increasingly aware of the thick cluster of people that had formed around us. *"Tang?" "Tang?"* Heads shaking. More staring. Discussion in Chinese.

"Come on, let's get out of here." I needed no further encouragement. Back on the street I took a deep breath.

Ken would have to drink his tea without sugar.

In a Japanese Home

Angela and Stefan have made friends with two Japanese, the only other children in our building: Mizuki, age twelve, and her eight-year-old brother Ryo. They live two floors below us, but we seldom see the family; both children are in school until midafternoon, the father spends most of the day in classes and none of them join us in the cafeteria because the mother, Inoko, cooks the family meals. But neither their socially withdrawn lifestyle nor the language barrier nor the pressure on Ryo and Mizuki to study hard and perform with academic excellence in the Chinese schools has prevented the children from enjoying their late afternoons together.

Yesterday I went down to talk to Inoko, to make sure Angela and Stefan weren't imposing. As is the custom, I went in house slippers and bowed as she motioned me to come in. She had been involved in a card game with the children which she now left to bid me welcome. I thought again how charming she looked. Her big brown eyes expressed a mixture of shyness and good will, radiating a motherly warmth and trustworthiness. Slowly, with a lot of guessing and gesturing, we told each other our age, how long we would be in China, and what grades our children were in. "My English . . ." she stammered and shook her head, embarrassed not to recall more of what she had learned in school a long, long time ago. I understood how she felt. I regretted as much that I did not know any Japanese. Here again was a potential friend that would remain out of reach because of the language barrier.

"How do you communicate?" I asked Angela when she came back upstairs after two hours of card games.

"Oh, it's just some version of 'Old Maid' we've been playing. It's easy to figure out."

"Does anyone speak English?"

"The father knows some, but he isn't around most the time. Mizuki can say a few words. It doesn't matter. We get along without words."

"What do you play besides cards?" "Yesterday we played featherball outside, but not for very long. Mizuki had to get back to studying. She seems to have a lot of homework to do all the time."

"Would you like to go to Chinese school?"

"Yeah. I think it'd be fun."

Ken and I have been thinking of enrolling Angela and Stefan in public school. It would keep them occupied and allow them to meet Chinese children their own age. Who knows, maybe they would even pick up the language more quickly than we. There is an elementary school with a large yard and some play equipment just across the street to the east of our campus. Every morning at ten o'clock music blasts through the loudspeakers outside. From our balcony we can watch the children tumble out of the building and line up to exercise. *Eee, Ar, San, Se,* counts the leader while the kids stand in four neat rows making their precisely patterned motions.

It would be a unique experience for our children to attend school here. Even if they couldn't understand the instructions at first, I am sure they would gradually pick up what is going on just by imitating their classmates. We need to find some way of breaking through the social isolation that is caused by the language barrier. But are public schools open to Americans? On the other hand, if Mizuki and Ryo can go, other foreigners may be able to attend as well.

2

Some Cultural Differences

Building Projects, Housing and Administrative Hassle

Ever since we arrived, a group of about two dozen workers from the countryside have been digging the foundation of what is to become the new residence hall for foreign students. In anticipation of a long-term open-door policy in China, the institute is planning to have students from Europe, the United States, Canada, and Japan who want to study Chinese at Dalian, all of whom need special housing. The building we presently live in will be reserved for foreign faculty members and exchange program directors. Governmental regulations determine which guests are assigned what type of accommodation. "Foreign experts" have the highest standing; then come those with lesser degrees, called foreign teachers; then foreign students, the Chinese faculty, and, finally, Chinese students. That's quite a hierarchy for a supposedly classless society!

We are wondering what the housing for future foreign students will turn out to be like. Undoubtedly their rooms will be superior to those of their Chinese classmates; but it is equally clear that they will not have nearly the comfort that our group has enjoyed this semester.

It has been fascinating to watch the progress on the building. For weeks, the workmen have dug up earth with nothing but shovels and picks, patiently moving dirt pile after dirt pile out of the way. How quickly this work could have been accomplished with modern equipment! Here, short of making the bricks, everything is done by hand.

Will the workers receive a special bonus if the building is completed by the target date, August 15? Probably so. Why else would they be so amazingly diligent, working day and night? Right now, in the chilly February air, it is a special hardship. I wonder how they stay warm in the primitive brick shelters they have erected in a U-shape at the edge of the football field. From our window on the fifth floor we can see the women hanging up the wash to dry and gathering it up again half-frozen. The group is a small community by itself; they don't interact much with the Chinese employees in our building. They know they are here only for this one project, like migrant workers without much social standing in the larger society.

Angela and Stefan are catching a glimpse of preindustrial working conditions. This is the way people used to construct houses for centuries, relying merely on manual labor and simple tools. At home we would never see anything like this.

"Did you know a construction worker was killed here shortly before you came?" Jacques told us one evening over dinner. The team had been assigned to tear down an old brick building. They had hammered away at the brick with their picks until the wall crumbled and crushed one of the workers as it fell.

"My students watched it happen," said Claudine. "They heard the noise from their classroom and rushed to the window. It was just before their winter break."

It had taken several hours to remove the partially buried corpse, and the spattered blood remained for days. Many of the students were outraged by the incident and heavily criticized the backwardness of their country, demanding to know why huge buildings had to be torn down and rebuilt by hand, with practically no protection for the workers.

"Life doesn't count for anything here." Claudine used the opportunity to come down hard on what she called the "Chinese system."

"You can say that again!" Jacques agreed. "They shove people around whenever they feel like it. Look what happened to the dean and now to Monsieur Chou."

"What about them?" I asked.

"Well, you know they are into 'modernizing' the campus right now, wanting to build that new high-rise for foreign students. To make room, a whole row of small brick houses had to be torn down, and the former residents had to put up with makeshift arrangements. The dean and his family were moved into a room in the English Department."

"You mean a classroom?"

"Yes."

"But that's only temporary, isn't it? I thought they are working on new faculty housing, too."

"Wait till you hear about Chou, though," Claudine continued. "He's my colleague in the French department, a really nice older man. He and his wife refused to move as quickly as they had been told. They had made other plans for the weekend.

Well, while he and his wife were gone, the construction workers were told to take the roof off his building. When he returned, the snow was blowing in."

"It happened to be one of the coldest nights of the month, too," added Jacques, "with a blizzard raging. Somehow they survived until the next day and moved in a hurry. Claudine and I went over to help them. I took my camera and told one of the administrators I wanted to be sure to capture on film how they were treating their employees. That didn't go over too well."

"We invited them over for a meal that next day and even asked Chou and his wife to stay with us overnight," said Claudine. "But it's risky for a Chinese to accept help from foreigners. They would have been stigmatized. Temporarily it would mean less inconvenience, but later on they'd hear about it."

"What do you mean, hear about it?"

"Be criticized, get less pleasant courses to teach, not be advanced professionally . . . who knows."

Again the conversation with Claudine and Jacques left me with considerable unease. I have no reason to doubt their stories, but their picture of China seems so one-sided. I find myself wanting to caution them not to be so judgmental. True, the living conditions for construction workers are deplorable and the death of the one crew member was tragic. But how could it have been helped? The Chinese are trying to modernize as fast as possible. Some of the equipment and technology just aren't there yet. As for moving people into separate buildings, it was meant as a temporary solution; they would eventually end up with better housing. Maybe I am making up invalid excuses. But for me there is something distasteful about putting down our host country at every opportunity. Every time I hear China attacked, I ask myself whether similar injustices don't take place in our own nations. Are we as ready to stand up for the victims? Are we as ready to blame "the system"?

On the other hand, I am beginning to understand how Jacques and Claudine feel. Last week they lost a major battle to obtain better housing for themselves by moving into a larger apartment in another wing of our building. A single Japanese teacher had occupied it and was returning home. Early in the morning Susan, the Hopkins, Claudine, and Jacques gathered in the apartment to say good-bye and "claim the space" like squatters.

At first the foreign housing administrator thought it beneath himself even to talk to them. Claire, who later told me the details of the confrontation, was outraged by the disrespect implied in the refusal to listen. Gradually he moved so far as to inform them that another Japanese man had been assigned the apartment and would move in within the next two hours. Three rooms, kitchen, and bath for a single man! What was it that made him deserve the privilege? After a lot of hedging, he informed Jacques and Claudine that the Japanese delegation had stipulated the apartment in the contract with the language institute.

"They know how to play by the rules," Claudine said, furious. "No one told us what to ask for before we came. Everything has to be nailed down in black and white. If we'd ever come here again (which of course we won't), we'd make sure every detail from square footage to book shelves and kitchen supplies is written down."

In a different context, the issue might have been dismissed as minor, but in China status and respectability correspond to size of housing, so Claudine and Jacques saw the rejection of their request as an indication of their worthlessness in the eyes of the Chinese. Already upset with their stay, they saw this event as the last straw.

I have been here long enough now to know that Chinese bureaucracy gnaws away at a foreigner's patience until we are all ready to blow up. Just two days ago I had my own big confrontation with the housing administrator. Ever since our arrival we have had to bicker and beg for basic furniture. When we first moved in we had seen five collapsible beds folded up and stored in one of the rooms. We had decided to keep one of the additional beds in the livingroom to use as a couch during group meetings; but we soon learned we weren't the ones making the decisions. All the beds but three were removed. "Why can't we use one as a couch?" we asked. "The beds are not for sitting on," said the housing administrator. "Do you really mean we can't sit on the beds?" I asked, incredulous. Li, who served as translator, repeated that yes, indeed, we could not sit on them. Of course I knew very well that all Chinese use their beds as couches during the daytime. The argument was so ridiculous that even Li, whose face is usually an unintelligible mask, turned red.

This was just the beginning. Later the same day we were told that the fan we had brought over from another apartment had to be taken back. Again, we asked our naive "Why?" which never leads anywhere. Li said we were getting an additional bookshelf, and so we couldn't have the fan. Thinking of the sweltering heat in the summer months, I replied that the fan had been promised to us earlier.

"It has to be one or the other," said Li, making me feel like a kid in a candy store. "You can't have both."

"All right, then we'll keep the fan and forego the bookshelf," we said. But by then Li was on the phone consulting with the housing administrator who indeed confirmed that we could not have the fan.

When the next fuss was raised over a couple of cups and a towel I had brought from the other apartment, I lost my patience. Unable to put up with any more petty harrassment, I yelled at Li, "All right, we'll just buy the furniture we need by ourselves. But don't expect us to donate any of our books to the library. Every single book will be shipped back to the United States, along with our other belongings, and our own administrators will hear about the way we have been treated. You can count on it."

I totally lost control. Since I couldn't bear to stay in Li's presence, I rushed downstairs to Claire's apartment and broke down sobbing and shaking with anger. How amazing that he managed to put me in such a rage! When I came to my senses, I began to tell myself that Li was just a small official around here, under the thumb and totally at the mercy of a superior who in turn depended on the grace of another higher-up.

When I got back upstairs Ken related that Li had become very apologetic after my outburst. Apparently part of the problem is that certain equipment is assigned to specific rooms and should not be moved from there. We have been promised two additional arm chairs in place of the couch, and conceivably fans will be purchased for all the foreign teachers later in the year. So in a sense I won the battle, but it was a Pyrrhic victory. I can hardly believe how passionately and childishly I reacted. In an Asian context, where control of emotions indicates maturity, I had lost face by flying into a rage. My relationship to Li, I am sure, is irreparably damaged, but I'll live with it. What I resent most of all is that he pushed me into acting like an imbecile when a simple explanation about the room policy would have clarified matters.

On Language Acquisition

"How many characters have you learned?" our Chinese students ask after class. On the surface the question is innocent enough. They are interested in the progress of our language study. But underneath there rings doubt that we have gotten very far. Chinese are convinced that their language is the most difficult on earth, and they may be right.

"Thirty or forty," I say, recalling the efforts of the past week. The students laugh. A literate Chinese person knows three thousand, and at least eight hundred are needed to begin reading Chinese publications.

"We focus more on the spoken language," I say in self-defense, annoyed to see our understanding of Chinese reduced to nothingness.

"Oh, but you can't learn Chinese without studying the characters."

"Why not? Don't small children manage to speak Chinese before they learn to read? We are picking up words fairly quickly now, even though we don't know what they look like on paper."

"I don't think it would work." The students look doubtful.

"Well, I taught European languages with that method to people who wanted to go abroad and learn basic conversation very quickly. Believe me, it *does* work."

"Say something in Chinese for us!"

Hesitatingly, I rehearse some of the phrases from our book. The students smile and clap their hands. They are genuinely pleased, even though I have undoubtedly made pronunciation errors. It is fascinating for them to see foreigners struggle with their language. The question "How many characters have you learned?" was not meant to be sarcastic. They posed it not to highlight the futility of our undertaking nor to make fun of our slow progress. I imagine they just wanted to find out how much we have already become part of their world. They are excited to see us try and want to invite us into that world.

I have noticed a growing familiarity with Chinese. It is not that my vocabulary is all that vast. But when we first arrived in Dalian, the sounds blended together like the confusing noise of a tuning orchestra. Now I am beginning to isolate words within sentences. I can tell whether I am listening to Chinese or Japanese. I can pick out *meiguo ren* (American) when my friends introduce me. I know how to ask for prices in the store, and I can understand the answer if it is given slowly. When the Chinese talk together, I listen for words I already know and can sometimes figure out what they are discussing.

"How many characters have you learned?"

Not many. But I won't let the question irritate me. Chinese is learnable, even if it takes time.

Meeting Xiao

"Ingrid, would you and Ken come down for a bit?" Claire called from a floor below. "Cao Shengli is here and has brought some of his paintings. I want you to meet him."

Claire's whole living room was covered with art work. Large silk screens painted with water color were tied with string to the water pipes near the ceiling. Calligraphy scrolls hung over the doors. Smaller square pictures of plants and birds sat on the chairs and sofa. In a corner, engrossed in a conversation with the pipe-smoking Simon, stood the artist, a short man of undefinable age with glasses and a receding hair line.

"This is Cao," said Claire, presenting her friend. "Hello. Pleased to meet you," he said politely and shook hands with us before resuming the dialogue with Simon.

"And this is his friend, Xiao Guodong. He is also an artist but he specializes in wood engravings. Someday you'll have to bring your work for a display in our building. Will you?" she asked Xiao Guodong as he rose from the corner of the couch. He was about six inches taller than Cao. His masculine face with its pronounced cheek and jawbones and very narrow eyes lost its hardness when he smiled.

"Yes, I would like to." He looked at us. "Do you teach English here at the Foreign Language Institute, like Claire and Simon?"

We told him about our efforts to learn Chinese, our English conversation classes, and our special task as first directors of an ongoing exchange program. He listened with interest.

"Can anyone apply to participate?"

"No, I am afraid not. Only teachers from the Institute get to go overseas, in exchange for our students coming here."

"Oh," he said, a bit disappointed. "It sounds like a very good program."

"Where did you learn to speak English so well?"

"I apologize for my many mistakes," he said, making me cringe. Will Chinese people ever be able to admit their talents without first putting themselves down? There was no doubt he was fluent in the language.

"No, really," I forced myself through the polite ritual of humility. "I haven't heard you make a single mistake. Who taught you?"

"My father, mainly, who was a teacher. But I also listen to the radio a lot while I work. We can get BBC and also "Voice of America." I know a few people who have picked up the language on their own. Have you been to the "English Corner" in Labor Park on Sunday afternoon? People come there to practice speaking English and to learn from others."

"Do you go there?"

"Seldom."

"Then how do you keep up your language skills?"

"It's a problem. There are not many foreigners around. I know a few foreign teachers from Dagong University, but mainly I just practice with the radio and books."

"Why do you want to perfect your English?"

"Someday I hope I can go to America, maybe, if there is interest in my art work."

"That's what they'd all like to do," said Claire who had overheard part of the conversation. "I don't mean that as a criticism," she added quickly when she noticed Xiao's face darken. "In fact, I'd love to help you get a clientele over there, both you and Cao. We ought to have a display like this once a month and invite all the foreign teachers to come look at your work. When Simon and I go back to the States, maybe I can take some pictures and wood carvings along to sell."

Xiao nodded but didn't comment. I moved on to admire Cao's paintings. Susan, who had come in a few minutes earlier, had fallen in love with a rough landscape of rocks and trees on a light blue silk backing.

"How much is this one?"

"Please ask Claire," was Cao's brisk reply. Like many artists, he seemed not to like putting prices on his creations. Claire apparently was taking over the role of his manager, wanting to protect her Chinese friend from giving away his masterpieces at ridiculously low prices.

"Do you think we could afford to buy some?" I asked Ken.

"Sure, but why don't we wait until later in the year. Which ones do you like best?"

"The set of four over there." I pointed to a series of watercolors depicting the four seasons, each cheerful and fresh, yet masterfully simple in their design.

"Cao prefers his calligraphy," said Claire. "But I agree with your choice. Those would sell easily in the United States, I think. The lettering doesn't mean as much to people over there; and yet it's so much more Chinese. I've come to like it a lot."

"May I look at your wood carvings some day?" I turned back to Xiao who had withdrawn into a corner.

"Yes, of course."

"I'd love to see them, too," said Susan.

"You are both welcome."

"Where is your studio?" I persisted, wanting to make sure he knew my interest was genuine.

"If you like I can pick you up and take you there."

"How about next Wednesday, Susan, when our students have their political meetings? Would that suit?"

We agreed to meet at 3 p.m. in front of the theater at the foot of the hill.

A Bible Course

Who would have thought that at a language institute in China a foreign teacher would receive permission to teach about the Bible? Susan McLean, I recently learned, is a former Catholic nun who made a convincing argument for the school authorities that an introduction to biblical literature is vital for understanding the great literary works of Western culture. Susan left her order a few years ago when she felt a strong call to go to China but found no support among her superiors at the convent. Determined that China was her mission field, she closed the door on her thirty-year career as a nun and headed out on her own.

She came as an English teacher, knowing that modern China would not tolerate missionaries. Yet her lifestyle and thinking are much the same as they were in the convent. Her apartment is strikingly simple and impeccably clean; no pictures adorn the plain white walls. On her neatly made bed, propped up against the pillow, sits a crucifix. Her bookshelf is filled with Catholic reading material, all neatly arranged with not a single book sticking out further than the rest. Rumor has it that when her paycheck comes, Susan, who seldom handled money before, pedantically separates the cleaner-looking bills from the shabby ones, using the latter to cover her expenses while saving up the pretty kind. She lives on an absolute minimum and, in her obsession with bargains, is more frugal than the Chinese themselves.

By now, Susan has taught two sessions of weekly class, "The Bible in Western Literature." Not surprisingly, she has already been called in and criticized that there is too much emphasis on the Bible. Susan thinks that five to ten students have been deliberately planted in the lecture hall in order to report on the content of her classes.

To some extent, I can see both sides of the issue. The Chinese want to make sure that there is no proselytizing and yet Susan throws herself into the course with whole-hearted evangelistic fervor. The criticism that the first two sessions were entirely biblical is valid. During the first meeting Susan went over the various books of the Bible, giving a structural and historical overview as well as an indication of what the Bible has meant in Western culture. The second week she talked about the Christian understanding of God and the trinitarian formula. Rather daringly she concluded the class with a challenge: "You say that there is no God, but I want you to try the following. Every day for the next three weeks, say, 'God, I don't know you. But if you do exist, I would hate to spend the rest of my life without knowing you. So if you are real, let me know you.' "

I think that this could have been (and was) rightfully interpreted as an attempt to Christianize the class. When Susan was called in to justify herself, she said she had only had two lectures, during which she needed to lay the foundation for the rest of the course. She had to begin with the biblical teaching. How else would it be possible to understand a work like "Paradise Lost" or "The Scarlet Letter"? The students, when she asked them, didn't know anything about the Bible. They had never heard of Abraham, Moses, the Exodus, or the meaning of the cross.

Moreover, to reverse the order and begin with the literary work and go back to the biblical source was impossible because of the study conditions here. The student library held at most one copy of the literary work, if any. To place some documents in their hands for study, Susan had to ask the department secretary, who does not understand English, to type on a stencil the entire Gospel of Mark and a few other passages of the Bible that Susan considered crucial for her course. At least the students will have this much material to work with.

It will be interesting to see what comes of the controversy. The course might well be cut entirely if the reports continue to be critical. I have decided to attend from now on to test the validity of what is being said and perhaps to glean a reaction from some of the students' faces. Susan says some students have talked to her individually outside of the class. Her happiness makes me think that the underlying motive for the class is indeed missionary zeal. To protect her and the students, I suggested she give an overview of the course at the beginning of the next lecture. If the observers get to see on the blackboard that literary works will indeed be considered soon, they may have fewer objections.

In Susan's opinion there is nothing the officials seem more afraid of than the teaching of the Christian faith. Aside from sexuality one can discuss almost anything, including governmental policies or societal mores. Why the apprehensiveness about religion? I don't think it is suspicion of Western influence. More likely, governmental funds might be cut or the power structure inside the Institute could be changed in order to achieve greater compliance with governmental policies.

In Class with Susan

Late for the lecture, I peek through the window in the door of the large hall. A mass of Chinese faces look in my direction, but not at me. The hall is packed with at least 200 students. I squeeze through the door, hoping to find a seat somewhere and not to create a disturbance.

Hardly anyone notices. They are all absorbed in Susan's lecture. Toward the back I find a place on a bench next to a student I recognize from one of my own classes.

Susan is lecturing on the Trinity. Why is she starting with so difficult a concept, hard even for Christians to comprehend? The students listen intently as she illustrates the Oneness of God in three persons with the analogy of water, ice, and steam: one substance, different forms. Then she tells the story of St. Augustine and the little boy on the beach. Susan's students smile and nod. Like all of us, they are captivated by legends and illustrations. To back up her teachings about the Trinity with scripture, she reads John 1:1–4; John 14:1–4; Mark 1:9–13; Colossians 1:15–18; Ephesians 1:3ff., 3:14–19; and Acts 2:1–4. The students follow eagerly in their "Bibles." Just today they have received the books: a compilation of important passages including the complete Gospel of Mark. The volume is full of mistakes, with no indication of verses, the text reproduced on hair-thin paper that one can breathe through. But the students now have at least excerpts of the Bible in their own hands. That is, some of them do. Susan had asked for 250 copies, but only eighty were made. On the bench where I sit, no one has a copy.

It touches me deeply to see the students so hungry for resource materials. During the break Susan hands out sheets with literary texts: poems by Donne, Hopkins, and Herbert. Two hundred arms reach eagerly for the sheets, afraid there again might not be enough copies. This time there are enough, but the secretaries have forgotten to put some of the page numbers and titles on, so that it is hard to find the right text. As best I can, I help out the students in my row.

The poetry is way above the students' heads. Donne's "Batter My Heart, Three-Person God, for You," would have been difficult even for my "Introduction to Literature" students back in the United States. Susan explains patiently: "The poet says, 'so far, God, you have only knocked at my heart. But I am too stubborn. I want to keep shutting you out. So please batter my heart. Force your way in. Don't give up on me.' " Through her interpretation, Susan is again evangelizing and fighting ideological walls which she presumes bar the students' way to God.

In the second hour, Susan deals with creation as God's outpouring of love into the universe. To my great relief, she does not insist on reading the story as historical truth. She explains that biblical writers didn't research facts. They were more like poets, charming their readers, seeking to convince them not through accuracy, but through beauty. The writers were not scientists interested in evolution. What they cared about was the religious implication: not *how* things came into existence, but *who* was the source of all life.

Susan then talks about the literary structure of the first creation story with its repetitions, refrains, and couplets which give the passage rhythm and cadence. For the use of the Genesis story in art she refers to Connelly's *Green Pastures,* Milton's *Paradise Lost,* and Michelangelo's painting of God's finger touching Adam. How much time it would take to go into detail! But at least the students are getting a sense of how deeply Western culture has been shaped by biblical teachings. For Susan, the references to the abundance of literary works using the biblical themes serves a double purpose. She can convince the monitors that she is indeed teaching literature rather than just Bible. At the same time, the literary work reinforces what she has said about a given scriptural passage, so that in a sense the students are getting a double dose of Christian teaching.

I am intrigued by the class, especially by Susan. Meek and gentle in appearance, even in the way she speaks, she nonetheless has great energy, determination, and charisma. She also has a knack for explaining difficult concepts in simple ways. I am reaping unexpected benefits from the course because students are beginning to ask me faith-related questions. Today the person next to me on my wooden bench wanted to know during break whether Jesus was God. I explained the orthodox position of "fully human and fully divine," which defies all logic for people who see the two as totally contradictory. Then he asked me to explain a phrase from last week's lecture: "I am who am." I told him about the power of naming things, and that we are not to define, that is limit, God according to our own imagination. He seemed satisfied with the answer. I wanted to continue by explaining that the *am* has been understood as eternal presence: "I am with you now, as I have been and will be." But the lesson continued.

School Enrollment and New Priorities

The children have begun attending public school. It took a while to make the arrangements, but since elementary education is compulsory for children here, we had no problem with attaining special permission from the city government to enroll ours. Li and his supervisors helped with the red tape. They either forgot about our recent unpleasant encounter or decided this was a favor they could grant more easily since it did not conflict with regulations. I need to keep telling myself that many official actions do not stem from personal animosity toward foreigners but, rather, are the result of a complex system of rules and relationships toward superiors that an outsider has difficulty deciphering. It bothers me that administrative actions are perceived as favors. Most get done eventually, but the speed and efficiency varies greatly according to whether an official *wants* to help. Thus it is wise, in the long run, to butter up those who hold power. I resent it on principle, but even more so because as a speechless foreigner I cannot plead my own case and am utterly dependent on others for making arrangements.

Anyway, Angela and Stefan are in school now. The Chinese teachers decided to put them both in first grade because the textbooks are better illustrated and Chinese characters are studied on a more elementary level. I understood the reasoning but was somewhat concerned about the social implications of placing them with much younger children. Having observed classes for a day, I realize now that it was a good choice. There is little interaction between students during the class period anyway; and during the breaks they can freely intermix with the older children.

With Angela and Stefan gone every morning, I need to reassess how I can make the most out of my stay here in Dalian. The basic decision is whether or not to continue the intensive Chinese language course. My goal is to learn as much as possible about China in the short five months I have left. I realize that in-depth knowledge of a foreign people can seldom be reached without living in their midst and speaking their language. But at the same time I am aware that even if I did nothing but study Chinese all day long between now and our departure, my conversational skills would be rudimentary. To get an impression of what people really think and feel, I would still have to rely on those who speak English.

Skipping the Chinese classes would give me four free mornings per week to write while the children are in school. The afternoons and evenings would then be left for explorations that in turn supply more material to write about. The people back home in Indiana are eager to see the people of China the way I have seen them, and for that, rather than study vocabulary drills, I need to go look at faces, shop downtown, stroll through alleys, and observe interactions. There is a limit to what one can say about a Chinese class, but possibilities to discover new things while walking around are endless.

What I have in mind is this. The Chinese students of English are very eager for time with native speakers to practice their language skills. So is Xiao, the artist, whose studio I visited last week. They will all be glad to take me for walks through Dalian. On the way, we will speak English the whole time. I will ask them about things I see that strike me as curious, and they can explain. They get to improve their language ability while I learn about China. I'd like for someone to translate the signs on the street and the texts of posters. I want to know about the strange foods that are sold in the open market. I'd like to see a typical Chinese home on the inside. And, more than anything, I want to get to a deeper level of sharing with Chinese persons. Since I only have five months left, these individuals will necessarily be the ones who know English.

But I am still scared of dropping out because the decision is so final. Is there no way to do both the language study and the rest? No, I think not. There are three other classes I want to attend, which take up six hours total. One is "China Today," which teaches me many things about the way the Chinese feel about their country. Another is "Taiji," an opportunity for exercise as well as a door to the Chinese tradition and soul. And finally, there is Susan's Bible course. Already the Chinese students have begun asking me faith-related questions in order to understand the points of the lecture.

I simply cannot afford to pass up these opportunities. In my circumstances, learning about China has to come first; learning the language is secondary.

Tidbits from "China Today"

Our "China Today" class provides opportunity to ask almost anything we want to know about modern China. Over the course of a day, I come up with dozens of questions. If I have a pencil and paper handy, I jot them down and take them to class with me. One thing that has always puzzled me is the number of different names for Dalian. I had seen it listed as Dairen and Talian on older English maps. When my father tried to locate the city in his German atlas, all he could find was Luda. Teacher Wang finally clarified matters for me. Darien, he explained, was the name given to the city by the Russians when they occupied it from 1945–1954. Dalian is the Chinese name, made official in 1949. Talien is a way of writing the same name according to an earlier phonetic system. Before 1949, there were two cities in this area: Dalian and Lushun. When they were administratively united, officials combined elements of both names and called the place Luda. But the new name never caught on among the local population. In the early sixties, Lushun became a district of the city, and around 1980 the name was changed back to Dalian.

We often learn about local history from Wang. Recently he explained why there is such strong anti-Japanese feeling in this area. During the Second World War, the Japanese occupied three provinces of Northeast China. They plundered homes, burnt villages, and exterminated vast numbers of Chinese. Thirty thousand were killed in Dalian alone. Many of our students from this province (Liaoning) have grandparents who were born on the other side of the Yellow Sea and moved here after the war because the original population has been killed.

Among the older generation anti-Japanese feeling is still strong because of the massacres. When a few years ago a Japanese government official came to visit, the resentment against flying the Japanese flag was so high that the leaders had to call special meetings to explain that the Japanese were their friends now. The younger people feel less hostile because they did not experience the war. Even so, there are periodic anti-Japanese demonstrations to commemorate the suffering under the occupation.

Interestingly, the Chinese talk about World War II as the "War Against the Japanese Aggressors" (1937 to 1945). History lives in the minds of a people, and thus it takes on a certain national perspective. World maps for sale in downtown Dalian feature China in the center, as the Middle Kingdom, whereas students in the United States unfold the world map so that China ends up on the far left. Each nation tends to put itself in the middle of the universe, and from that position world politics is perceived.

Wang's most fascinating lectures concern China's recent past. Last week he told us about the so-called "Great Leap Forward," initiated in 1958, which was based on the assumption that communism had arrived in China. Communal kitchens were established all over the country. With fervent patriotism people destroyed their private kitchenware in an attempt to show community spirit. Because of climatic conditions and human administrative error, the three years from 1960 to 1962 were economically disastrous. Afraid to be seen as critical of the government, leaders in the countryside reported to Beijing that conditions were good; but, in fact, prices were going up and few had enough to eat. To stay alive, people in rural areas ate leaves from the trees and cobs without the corn. Intellectuals who visited the countryside and were daring enough to report the truth were imprisoned and silenced.

I wonder sometimes how much Wang can tell us. Politically, he is walking a tightrope. He carefully weighs his answers before he gives them. Sometimes he laughs, a bit embarrassed, and changes the topic. He is conscious of the volatile political climate of China's recent past. The Cultural Revolution has taught intellectuals that it does not pay to be openly critical of one's leaders. Wang knows he has to be careful, especially around a group of short-term foreign residents who little comprehend what consequences he might face if he trusts us too much.

On the other hand, it is acceptable now to criticize the policies of the last ten years under Mao. While the 1978 constitution still praised the Cultural Revolution and declared private ownership illegal, China's latest constitution has a distinctly different tone. It allows private ownership, reconverts communes into town and cities, and says nothing favorable about the 1966–1976 period. Even in the media the Cultural Revolution is now described as a horrible mistake. And so it is not uncommon to find students and teachers willing to talk about the hardships of that period.

However, their tone is one of regret and vulnerability, not anger or disdain. People have become careful. Victimized during the Cultural Revolution, they are leery of criticism and counter-criticism. They know that any radical trend will evoke a reaction on the other end of the political spectrum. For stability's sake, and to save their own heads, the present leaders have been wise in making fundamental changes quietly and gradually. There was no boisterous public condemnation, no attempt to turn the world upside down overnight. With the new administration has come an opening toward the West, admiration of private initiative, and a generally higher standard of living all over China. People agree that Deng's government is very popular. A key to Deng's success is that he lacks the extremism of the earlier leaders.

Wang is typical of his generation. He wants to be careful, yet open at the same time. Like Xiao, he seeks Western friends; but he also knows that they will leave again in a short while, whereas he has to spend the rest of his life in China and may be held accountable for what he says. I give him credit for trusting us as much as he does.

Our ignorance about Chinese affairs allows us to ask questions others might consider naive. "Why do so many people prefer to live in the city?" we wondered after Wang had told us that from 1964 to 1983 the population in urban areas increased by 62 percent.

"Living conditions in the country are rough," Wang said. "Homes in most villages have no central heating, running water, or electricity. The transportation system is bad, limiting access to consumer goods, hospitals, and schools. In the cities, where food is supplied by the government, people can purchase rice and flour with ration cards and find a much greater variety of vegetables, fruit, and meats. In the country, most of the food is grown locally. Depending on the region, there may be only one kind of staple food.

"Moreover, in the countryside people are expected to find their own jobs. The government does not assign a work place, and job opportunities in the country are rare. The only choices are to be a farmer, a peddler, or a truck driver. Farmers have a hard life; their income is low, and they receive no free medical care and no bonuses. The merchants or shop assistants in the few private shops have trouble receiving and selling supplies because of the poor transportation system and the low income level of their customers. To be a truck driver is seen as the preferable option because drivers make the most money and are the most mobile."

I asked Wang how people managed to get out of the countryside.

"The easiest way is to become a college student," he said, "because the government will assign graduates a work place in the city."

"But wouldn't this create a 'brain drain' problem for the peasant class?" Asked Bob.

"I suppose it does," Wang agreed.

"Why isn't more effort put into decreasing the differences between city and country life?" Ken wanted to know.

"The government tries to do that, but it is difficult. People prefer living in the city not only because the country is underdeveloped, but also because they need to be within walking distance of their work place. If they had a car or a decent transportation system, they could drive back and forth like you do in America. But in the country few roads are good enough to drive on. Then also, cars are outrageously expensive in China. A new one costs 1,700,000 yuan, or a little under $60,000—as much as it costs to build a new primary school. People with a good job make only about 100 yuan a month, so no one can ever dream of buying a car."

"With China's dense population, wouldn't private ownership of cars lead to a horrible traffic situation anyhow?"

"That's what most foreigners think. But when one looks at the overall population in the province, it is only half that of West Germany for roughly the same area; and yet in West Germany almost every family owns a car."

We discussed suggestions of how one might turn the situation around, such as by starting to manufacture cars in China rather than importing them from Japan, or by developing the countryside through a better road system. For whatever reason this has not been seen necessary by the government, and so the countryside remains primitive.

Wang never tires of our questions. We keep bombarding him with our whys and wherefores, and the more we ask, the more questions arise. He probably finds it fascinating to look at his own country from our perspective and to learn about America by way of what we find fascinating. Chinese people don't ask "why." They are used to their own methods, styles, and behavior patterns. To be noticed, something has to be unusual.

Feather Bedding

In the small store at the foot of our hill, we can no longer purchase the produce directly from the person behind the counter. Instead of giving the money to the woman packing and weighing the fruit, one has to wait at a small booth, buy tickets for an amount to cover the purchase, and hand these tickets to the woman in charge of the fruit. The latter is well capable of handling money, for she gives out change if necessary. The only reason I can see for the complication is that it has created a new job. The process is bothersome for customers because we now have to stand in line twice: once to purchase tickets, then to obtain the food. This means a longer waiting period; moreover, the customer is forced to guess how many tickets to buy in order to pay for produce which has not yet been selected or weighed. Sometimes the price for full employment seems rather high.

Most state-owned enterprises in China are hopelessly overstaffed. Five or six people are assigned to one task, often rather trivial; instead of being expedited, the work process is slowed down with debates and consultations. Since people are often assigned to a job they don't particularly care for, they sometimes make attempts to take revenge. So it happens that occasionally persons are downright rude to customers. At those times we have to tell ourselves that if we were forced to labor wherever told, we would probably act the same way.

What Dreams May Come

Some of our students have had interesting dreams that reflect their struggle with culture shock. Lisa dreamed her eyes had changed shape so that she was unable to put her eye make-up on, no matter how hard she tried. Craig saw himself back home, wanting to communicate with his girl friend; but every time he tried to speak, only Chinese sentences would come out until his friend refused to have anything to do with him.

Early yesterday morning Claire called to tell me with a shaky voice that she had just woken up from a terrible nightmare. I rushed down to her apartment and listened to her story. In the dream she was at a Chinese restaurant with a group of American friends. She had ordered a meal for 2.50 yuan and was about to pay when the waiter insisted the cost was 3.10, handing her only 1.90 change for her five-yuan bill. A difference of 60 fen is nothing to get excited about. What made her angry was the sense of being at the mercy of others who were trying to give a nonnative speaker a bad deal. It was no longer a matter of 60 fen, but a matter of justice. It was a struggle against the frustration that becomes so overwhelming and pervasive as one confronts the Chinese structures.

"I know the meal costs 2.50. I read it in the menu," she argued.

"No, the one you ordered was 3.10."

"Show me the menu, and I'll prove it to you!"

"We don't have a menu."

Sure enough, no menu was to be seen anywhere. In broken Chinese, Claire began to scream. There had been plenty of menus before! Where were they hiding them? Her friends looked at her, embarrassed to watch her make such a fuss. This only increased her rage. An American woman in the next room, who put on an air of loving Chinese and understanding the culture much better than Claire, condescended to intervene. She went to the manager, who told her they didn't have any menus.

"You have to understand," she then explained to Claire, "that this restaurant doen't have menus. You can't expect too much."

"But I have seen one with my own eyes, and I ordered from it!"

The woman shrugged her shoulders and went away.

"I want my 60 fen. You owe them to me. I insist you give me my money back right now!"

The waiters pretended not to understand her. Claire said if they kept refusing the change, she would take it out of the cash register. Again, there was no reaction except innocent looks and blank smiles. Claire had had enough. Overcome with fury, she grabbled dishes from the table and smashed them on the ground. Then she started banging against an expensive metal door with her foot until it was bent all out of shape.

Suddenly they had a menu. No one knew where it had come from.

"See?" Claire exclaimed triumphantly. "There it says 2.50. Just like I told you!"

The waiter pointed to 3.10 scribbled just above it. "You were looking at the price for Chinese customers. The cost for foreigners is right here, 3.10."

Again Claire felt rage welling up inside her. There seemed to be no way to win the showdown. Finally, one of the Chinese said what was meant to be a compromise but turned out to be a last blow against her self-esteem: "Here, I'll just give you the sixty fen. But I must say, you are wrong."

That's when Claire woke up, in a sweat from fury, self-loathing, and frustration.

Stefan's Bout with Culture Shock

Ever since we came to China, Stefan has been the center of attention everywhere we go. People admire his blonde locks, his bright blue eyes, and his soft facial features. To them he is beautiful beyond belief, more so even than the babies they have on their wall calendars and their "one child only" posters. In the streets people turn their heads to look at him. Often they will make an admiring remark in passing, or they will stop and tell me directly how wonderful a boy they think he is.

At first Stefan relished the attention. He smiled at his admirers and let them take his picture. Physically affectionate by nature, he did not mind them stroking his head or putting their arms around him. But there came a point when the newness wore off. Gradually it began to bother him that he could never go for a walk without someone reaching over to touch his hair or bending down to get a close look at his face. While Angela felt badly neglected because her brother got all the attention, Stefan wanted nothing more than to be left alone. He talked of buying a wig, or shaving his hair, or wearing a hat. When people reached for him, he shrank back as if to avoid a beating.

Since the Chinese were simply expressing their good will and admiration, I tried to explain to Stefan that he had a great opportunity to contribute to international friendship simply by bearing it all with a smile. At the same time I understood his feelings. I knew how embarrassing it was for me to provoke curious stares everywhere I went, and I often walked quickly to avoid drawing a crowd. For Stefan the burden was even greater because people felt no inhibition to touch him.

The most difficult situation for Stefan to handle was the behavior of the Chinese on the public buses. It is the custom in China for adults to offer their seats to children. But Stefan loves to stand in the aisle and try to keep his balance while the bus is bouncing over potholes or going around curves. Every time we ride a bus, the same little drama unfolds. Inevitably someone gets up to offer him his seat. Stefan shakes his head or waves his hand in refusal. The Chinese, misinterpreting his reluctance as mere politeness, keep insisting. Even a loud and energetic *bu, bu, bu* (no, no, no) on his part only provokes more delight on the part of the other travelers who stretch their heads to get a better look of the cute little boy. I plead with him to accept, just to avoid a scene. Finally, after some arguing, he gives in and takes the seat, but he fights tears for the rest of the trip because the fun of riding the bus has been ruined once again.

Yesterday, after we had gone through another fruitless discussion about Stefan's feeling victimized, I finally came up with a story that seemed to help him put things in perspective.

"Imagine," I told him, "that a sweet little guy from Mars with a purple face and wiggly rubber horns came walking down the street in North Manchester. Creatures like that had been seen in the big cities for a few years, and people knew what they looked like from a number of television shows, but they never had seen a real live one before. And here he was, walking past their homes. Everyone in the neighborhood came out to take a closer look. They knew from television that Martians were basically friendly creatures, so they didn't hesitate to get close. Everyone reached over to touch the little horns wanting to know what they felt like. They asked him a question in English and were delighted to find that indeed he knew a few words, such as how he was and where he came from. So they tried to engage him in a longer conversation, but he didn't understand. To show their friendship they invited him for a ride in their car. But Martians are very scared of sitting in cars with humans. They would much rather wobble along on their own two feet and find out about life on earth in their own way. No one left them alone, and so they were unhappy. The people of North Manchester couldn't figure out why the Martians were wearing such a big frown underneath their purple horns. The more they tried to be hospitable, the more the Martians withdrew, until finally the people in town thought the Martians weren't friendly at all."

Stefan liked the story. One of his favorite pastimes is to fantasize about creatures from outer space. Whether the Martian will help him deal with his struggles on the bus and in the streets of Dalian remains to be seen; but at least now he has a little imaginary friend who understands how he feels.

3

Observations

On Crime

All the employees of the Foreign Language Institute have received free tickets to a Saturday afternoon movie called *World Regained,* about rehabilitation programs for Chinese juvenile delinquents. The film turns out to be highly entertaining, sentimental, and educational, at least for us foreigners. We are amazed to find the subject of crime addressed so freely in a public movie. The feature film is preceded by a black-and-white documentary about criminals recently arrested for murder, rape, smuggling, and other severe crimes. Gory in its details, it displays the mutilated victims, the weapons, and the places of the crime, without going into detail about motives. The objective is to stir outrage about this shame for the nation.

In the feature about the deliquent youth, corruption is portrayed as coming with Western influence. We are shown scenes of a group of teenagers watching X-rated video tapes. The Chinese around us in the movie theater click their tongues in dismay. The youth on the screen reach for cans of coke and throw their arms around members of the opposite sex, suggestive of an impending orgy. One of the boys takes his girlfriend to an expensive restaurant where they drink wine and eat with forks before he reaches for her leg under the table. Again the setting evokes visions of Western decadence.

In the rehabilitation center, the teenagers gradually evolve from corrupt criminals to model citizens ready to be returned to society as skilled workers. The change is brought about through the selfless dedication of social workers who inspire an ideal of upright living. Although I have no doubt that there are social workers in China, as in the United States, willing to give their lives to achieve a better future for deliquent children, the total absence of guards who have turned violent or of youth who have remained unchanged despite all efforts makes me question the realism of the film. There is an interesting twist at the end, though. When the woman social worker in the lead role returns home after a year at the rehabilitation center, she finds that her own son has turned criminal. For the Chinese, the woman carries no responsibility for this tragedy. As Westerners we question whether her long absence did not contribute to the boy's downfall.

Heart-wrenching scenes of mothers sobbing during the first reunion with their kids after months at the correction center; humorous dialogues with a street urchin arrested for pick-pocketing; realistic portrayals of public humiliation of criminals; scenes depicting deep respect for one's parents—all this makes the movie a fascinating cross-cultural experience.

Apparently the Chinese firmly believe that public exposure of unacceptable behavior is an effective deterrent. The same Saturday the movie is shown at the Institute, Jacques and Claudine see a truckload of criminals parade through Dalian. This humiliation must be a terrible experience in an Asian culture where it is so important to save face. Bob comments sarcastically that in the United States, where some crimes are committed just because they draw media attention, such a public display might not inhibit people too much. I am not certain. I can't help feeling sympathy for the person thus ridiculed, no matter how great the crime. Public humiliation strikes me as inhumane. In the States I have heard people say that if executions were public, our sensibilities would be so offended that the death penalty would be abolished. I am not sure about that either anymore. Here, the public can watch executions, and yet there seems to be little opposition to the death penalty. It is incurred easily, not just for murder and rape but also for procuring women, for any crime committed with a weapon, and even for theft involving over one thousand yuan.

Visiting a Middle School and a Local Restaurant

Alicia and I are fortunate to have made friends with English-speaking Chinese. Cheng, who is one of her literature students, knows Xiao well. Often the four of us go for walks together. As natives of Dalian, they not only know their way around but also have a keen sense of how to get things done. Yesterday they managed to show us a middle school. It was a major achievement, since in China "making arrangements" is a hopelessly bureaucratic process. Each action that could be seen as the least bit controversial requires lengthy consultations with people in charge. If foreigners are involved, permission has to come from higher up. Then, in order to show only the very best, the school would take days and days to prepare for the visit.

We don't care to see only the very best. We want to see a normal class in session, and so we have to take them by surprise. Xiao's future sister-in-law works as an English teacher in one of Dalian's middle schools. So we head out to pay her a visit. Xiao and Cheng go in first to talk to the headmaster. There is no guarantee that we'll be invited in; but sure enough, here he comes with our friends and welcomes us.

We find ourselves on a comfortable couch in the spacious office of the headmaster. Xiao explains we are from America. We all smile, and the conversation dies. With typical American directness, Alicia asks whether we could see a classroom. Xiao translates.

"The lunch break starts in ten minutes," we are told.

"That's all right," Alicia persists, "we just wanted to stop in for a little bit."

Negotiations in Chinese. Obviously, this is the way to proceed. Since it is too late to consult authorities, the headmaster has to decide on his own. And, luckily for us, the answer is yes.

Accompanied by Xiao's sister-in-law, the headmaster, Cheng, and Xiao, Alicia and I walk into an English class. After we are introduced, the students break into applause. In an effort to make a good impression, the teacher has her best student rehearse a passage memorized from their English textbook. While she calls on several others. I leaf through the book, which contains passages on Helen Keller, Karl Marx, and the Great Wall of China. Alicia whispers to Xiao that she would like to talk to the students. Xiao relates the message to the head master, who in turn informs the teacher (all in proper order!). Of course, Alicia is invited to speak.

In spite of her clear and slow enunciation, the students have trouble understanding her. In teaching foreign languages the Chinese place enormous emphasis on memorization and very little on active usage. Since Alicia and I are both interested in dialogue with the children, we invite them to ask questions about America in Chinese which our students can translate for us. Suddenly all inhibition is gone. They ask about the size of our classes, about subjects taughts, about favorite sports. Questions keep popping up until the bell rings. I promise them that when I get back to the States, I will tell school children there about this visit.

On our way out the headmaster says we are welcome to return for another visit any time. Both Alicia and I are eager to take him up on the invitation. I try to explain how they can reach us at the Foreign Language Institute if they want us to come back and talk longer to the classes. But the more concrete I become, the more noncommittal is the look on their faces. I suggest to Xiao on our walk to the trolley that perhaps I could show my slides from the United States to these middle school students some morning. He suppresses a smile. "Too complicated," he says. "You'd need permission, and I doubt they would even go so far as to ask the higher authorities."

Xiao and Cheng next take us to a Korean restaurant. "Strangely enough, most Chinese seem to prefer Korean food for their guests," Alicia fills me in quietly. "I'm not sure why." The place is an experience in going native. On the cement floor, surrounded by bare cement walls, stand four tables covered with bright-colored plastic cloth. At two of them, a group of Chinese are slurping their soup. The one next to the counter has been wiped clean, but for some reason our friends suggest the one closest to the street even though the floor all around it is covered with leftovers that people have spit out during the last meal: bones, shells, chewed vegetables, and bits of meat rejected for whatever reason. On the table cloth itself, spills and food bits add color to the flower design in a less than attractive manner.

Quite determinedly I insist we go to the free table at the back of the room. Our friends order beer, three dishes of shellfish, peanuts, and green peppers, and bowls with oriental spaghetti. While we wait, an attendant wipes up the spills on the other table and sweeps up the mess underneath as if it were the most normal thing in the world.

Our meal turns out to be delicious. It is hilarious to eat the foot-long noodles. Well-cooked yet firm, they cannot be cut into small parts. We wrap them around our chopsticks and just keep shoving them in, laughing and choking. The beer is served in soup bowls, either for lack of glasses or because that's just the way it's done. Alicia and I try all the different kinds of morsels, and our hosts are delighted to see that we are having such a good time.

After dinner Xiao takes us back to his studio. It is a small hut along the side of the street, with a display of his work leaning against the walls. Alicia, who has never seen him carve before, watches with fascination as he runs his small electric burner over the plywood. With a few quick strokes he creates an intricate landscape of mountains, trees, pagodas and bridges. I fall in love with a wood painting of rocks, boats, and hills near the seashore. Alicia has visited the place in Southern China, and so she asks for a duplicate. In less than twenty minutes, without looking once at the original, Xiao recreates it from memory and sells it to her at half-price.

What a good day it has been! I keep thinking how thankful I am for the friendship of Xiao and Cheng who keep unlocking so many doors for us. I wonder what I can do for them to show my appreciation. Al Deeter is coming in May; perhaps I could tell him to bring a present.

"Is there anything you would like from the United States?" I ask.

"Just keep speaking English with us," they say. "That's the greatest gift you can give us."

"How Are You?"

"How are you doing?" a friend writes in a letter. "Fine," I would have said had I met him on the street in North Manchester, and then we would have moved on to other subjects. But now we are in China. How are we doing? I suppose each person would tell a different story.

Stefan and Angela never had the opportunity to interact with so many adults who just love having them around. Angela spends many hours with Simon and Claire. Simon has taught her how to play backgammon and new card games and Claire has taught her how to make yogurt and peanut butter. Claire is an excellent cook; if I am lucky, some of her skill will rub off on my daughter.

Stefan also loves the Hopkins. This past week Claire took him to her college classes to give her students exposure to a real American boy. They all watched *The Black Stallion* together, a marvellous film with a creative little boy in the lead role. If the students expected our eight-year-old son to be as intriguing, they were not disappointed. He lectured to them about the latest theories on what caused the space shuttle to explode; about the AIDS epidemic and the transmission of germs; and about the trigger on a nuclear bomb. I was not in the class with them, but Claire gave me a stunning summary. Apparently Stefan relished having an audience for his theories.

Angela still feels pangs of jealousy on occasion but is beginning to realize that always standing in the limelight would eventually get on her nerves. Angela is by nature shy and withdrawn. She wants attention, but I think such over-abundance of it would soon become a burden to her.

The morning classes at the public school have turned out to be stressful. I had assumed the children would pick up Chinese fairly quickly but had underestimated two factors. First of all, in contrast to elementary classes in the United States, there is very little interaction among the children. They sit in straight rows facing front and are not allowed to talk to each other. Angela and Stefan learn more conversational Chinese during break and at play after school than they do during classes. Second, they cannot follow along in the textbook when the teacher or their classmates read. If the text were printed in pinyin or if they were learning a European language, they could locate the words easily even if they didn't understand their meaning, because the sounds would correspond visibly to the written word. Chinese, however, is not phonetic. A given word could be hidden anywhere among the 300 characters on a page. Thus Angela and Stefan are spending their mornings learning how to sit still and how a Chinese classroom is run. For us, this does not justify keeping them in school. We have therefore decided to terminate enrollment as of this weekend. Angela will begin tutoring her brother at home during the morning hours by working through the textbooks we brought from the United States.

One lasting benefit of their school attendance is that Angela and Stefan have made friends their age. Each afternoon as soon as classes end, six neighborhood children come over to play. Hesitant to enter the Foreign Experts Building, they call from five stories below. "Un-gee-laa!" "Sche-teee-fen!" For the next hour or two, unless we have other plans, the children play on the nearby athletic field. The games are noncompetitive, designed to develop skills and cooperation. A favorite is jumping in a sequence of well-designed steps over a long elastic band looped around two of the playmates. I am thrilled to see the children interact with such ease despite the language difficulty. Angela has learned several games and somehow manages to communicate almost everything she wants.

The Chinese students at the institute adore our children. They want them to come and be with them as much as possible. Angela and Stefan are thriving on being so appreciated. I am sure someday they will look back to these months as among the best of their lives.

So much for the children. What about the other members of our group? Peggy and Lisa are finding it difficult to adjust and are sometimes plagued with homesickness. They both have had upset stomachs and colds. Lisa spends enormous amounts on phone calls abroad, although she claims she now feels better about being in China than she did at the beginning. Peggy has asked a friend in America to send her some dark brown dye in order to do away with her reddish-blond hair. She can no longer stand constantly being stared at and having her hair fingered. The girls have not been too successful making friends with the Chinese, with the exception of Li who picked us up in Beijing when we first arrived. They feel more at home with some of the foreign faculty. To Li they relate in a playful, flirtatious, kidding sort of way that he apparently puts up with.

Bob and Craig have found ways to make their six months in China the exciting experience it should be. Craig is very interested in the traditional martial arts. He and Jacques get up at five-thirty several days a week to join the old people in Zhong Shan Square for their morning Taiji exercises. They also take private lessons from a Chinese woman and her son in a type of Taiji performed with a sword. Craig has purchased a beautiful sword at a special store in Dalian—quite a souvenir to take back home! Craig says he loves it here. He expected the facilities to be more like the rooms we had at the Beijing Sports College and finds that in comparison our accommodations are extravagant. It is all a matter of perspective. Bob spent last weekend in Beijing with Li. He is the most daring explorer among us. Like Craig and me, he relishes the exposure to a new culture. A good cook, he has given up eating downstairs in favor of preparing his own meals. This means frequent adventures with shopping at local markets, occasional bouts of diarrhea and upset stomachs, and many possibilities to surprise friends with home-cooked specialties. To each his own! I continue to enjoy Bob's easy-going nature, his humor, and his lucid comments on our various experiences.

A Letter About Country Life and Communism

To Tom, a member of my home congregation:

Yesterday evening I shared your letter with the students in my two English conversation classes at our institute. I know you had intended the letter for a farmer somewhere in the Chinese countryside, but meanwhile I have realized that such a correspondence could never come to be. Let me explain.

In China, life in the country is quite different from that in the city. Since there is no developed highway system, the country people live in relative isolation. From Dalian you have to go by train to the nearest town and then walk for miles and miles to reach a specific village. My friend Alicia, another teacher from our institute, and I will try a weekend trip to the countryside in about another month when it is warm enough to sleep in unheated buildings and the trees have turned green to bring out the full beauty of the land. One of our students has invited us to visit her grandmother in the country. If we are lucky, her brother-in-law will pick us up at the train station by truck and drive us for an hour over bouncy roads to our destination.

The people in the country are extremely poor. No one speaks English. Because of the massive literacy campaign since the revolution, they can read and write but only in Chinese. Their yearly income in some places is under $200, less than sixty cents a day. It is enough to buy food but not enough to pay forty cents for an air mail stamp.

So I decided to read your letter in class, where the students are familiar with basic English and know enough about China and the countryside to answer some of your questions. You cannot believe how excited they were about your letter. They hung on every word and crowded around the pictures to see you, Jill, and the children.

They could hardly imagine the size of your farm. Here, if I have understood the dimensions correctly, families are assigned only one acre, enough to feed themselves and produce a little to sell. In the South, where most of the rice is grown, they are paid a certain amount by government and thus are not dependent on the market. The financial figures you sent amazed them, especially the loss of 45 cents per bushel when you compared your cost with your gain. I explained that many farms have had to close in the last three years. In a sense the workers here have greater job security; on the other hand, their living and working conditions are primitive.

When we reached your paragraph on religion, the discussion became really bizarre. You had asked about their faith, and they told me that they believe in communism.

"If you said that to people in the United States," I replied, "they would be very shocked. Or they might think you are threatening."

"Why?" they asked, looking very surprised.

"In America we are taught that communism is evil."

"Really? Why do they think that?"

"I guess people imagine that under communism, their possessions would be taken away from them. Also, most of us are Christians, and communists don't believe in God; therefore, since we know that Christian values are good, we conclude communism must be bad."

"We have freedom of religion in China," they said. "It's in our constitution. You can be a Christian if you want to be." (I know this is true, because just last Sunday I attended a Protestant service in a church that was so crowded I could hardly get a seat.)

"But who among you is Christian or Buddhist?" I asked.

"No one," came the unanimous reply.

"And why is that?"

"To us those religions are superstitions."

"So tell me what you believe in!"

"We believe in the League, and in communism."

"What is the League?"

"It's a youth movement, for people age 14 and on until they are old enough to become party members."

"Can anyone join the League?"

"You don't decide to join. The people who are already in it select you. Only the very best, the kindest and the nicest, get chosen."

"What do you have to do to be good?"

"Help others. Be a model citizen. Be considerate. Don't be selfish."

"So it is an honor to be chosen?"

"Of course. And it is even more of an honor to become a party member. They make a lot of sacrifices and are very disciplined and righteous people."

"Can you choose *not* to become a party member?"

"Yes, you can. Many people do. It is tough to be a model citizen all the time. They don't want to put up with the discipline of being good."

I was almost ready to laugh. It sounded like someone following the call to be a monk or nun, except that of course party members can marry.

"When you tell Americans what you believe in, you better just say that you believe in kindness and in helping others. That, they can understand. But it would be furthest from their mind to associate this with communism."

Needless to say, we didn't get done with your letter. We'll continue reading it next week. I encouraged the students to write to you about China and promised to mail their letters to you myself. Perhaps someone will take us up on the invitation. It will be a wonderful opportunity to get to see things from their perspective. Your letter has been a great door opener to start our discussion on values. I look forward to sharing more of my own faith with them. I have a hunch that beneath the concepts of communism and Christianity, which sound so contradictory, we may find value systems that are not that vastly different. The other day an acquaintance summarized what it means to be a Chinese party member in the words of former President Kennedy: "Ask not what your country can do for you. Ask what you can do for your country." Amazing, isn't it?

4

Discoveries

New Discoveries and Growing Friendship

On our walks through Dalian's busy streets, Xiao and I frequently see a man covered with coal dust who is vigorously cranking a pitch-black, vase-shaped container over a metal box filled with glowing embers. In less than five minutes, popped rice explodes through the neck of the vase into an elongated sack of cloth. Children and adults come with pans and bowls to purchase the delicious snack.

"Don't try to eat it," says Xiao. I know from Alicia that it is the Chinese version of our popcorn. She too has advised me not to buy any because the primitive process of making it allows lead to get into the food. A number of people have died from lead poisoning. It is illegal to make the snack on the streets like this, but apparently it is a rather lucrative business. The health hazard has not decreased its popularity.

At the beach we meet fishermen who have worked all night gathering fish and seaweed from the ocean. That too is illegal, Xiao tells me, if the men have other jobs during the day. "Why can't they do with their free time what they want?" I ask.

"They can do what they like, except they shouldn't make extra money."

"Why not?"

In the United States, individual initiative like this would be admired. The diligence of these people is unbelievable. They have spent hours and hours fishing for a small batch of food that will bring them a net gain of perhaps six to ten yuan (three dollars). Why envy them the extra income? Time and again they have soaked their body in the ice-cold sea for this meager revenue. To me it seems they deserve all they can get for their labor.

Xiao is amused by my constant questions about why things are the way they are. Chinese people tend to go by the rules or find ways to circumvent them, but they don't ask too many questions. Those who break the rules have an excuse ready. We approach one of the fishermen to find out what he is planning to do with his catch. "It's for private consumption only," he lies to protect himself. Xiao translates, smiles, and later explains the situation in English.

"You could come back here by bike some time," I suggest to Bob who has accompanied us on one of our walks. Xiao acts surprised. "You bought a bicycle? What kind is it?" When he learns it is a Phoenix, the best one available in China, he whistles through his teeth and gets a thoughtful look on his face. Further along on our walk I explain to him that foreigners can buy Phoenix bikes at the Friendship Store.

"Are you allowed to pay in Renminbi?" he asks, knowing that the Friendship Store usually insists on Foreign Exchange Certificates.

"Not unless we have a White Card that identifies us as foreign workers who are paid with the regular currency. We may get a White Card later this year, but for now we have to use our tourist money. Would you like a Phoenix? I would be willing to buy it for you and let you pay me back in Renminbi."

I can tell Xiao is fighting with himself. On the one hand, he would really like such a bicycle. On the other hand, precisely because a Chinese rarely gets hold of a Phoenix, it would be obvious to his other friends and colleagues that he has had contact with foreigners.

"The situation in China may change again," he stammers o-bliquely, saying just enough to show that I interpreted his hesitation correctly. During the Cultural Revolution, when he was just a ten-year-old boy, he was forced to watch his mother being publicly criticized and paraded through the streets for having bourgeois tendencies. To this day the scene is ineradicably imprinted in his mind.

"Whatever you decide," I try to reassure him, "keep in mind that I will be gone in less than five months, whereas you are likely to live here for the rest of your life. Only think of what is best for you and your family. Don't let me influence you. But if you think it through and decide you want the bike, I'll be glad to get it for you."

Alicia said just yesterday that we will never be able to comprehend the Chinese, and for the most part I agree with her. But at this moment, on this walk, I think there has been true communication, marked by understanding and respect.

"Can you show me more of the campus?" I ask Song after class. We have lived here for two months now but have managed to stay blissfully ignorant of what life is like for Chinese students. We stay in our fancy Foreign Experts Building where we are served good food and have plenty of space in carpeted, wall-papered rooms.

"What would you like to see?" Song asks.

"How about your dorm room?"

"Oh, it's not clean right now. I'd better. . . ."

"I don't care if it's clean or not. My kids never clean up their room either. You'd have a hard time finding a perfectly tidy room in a dorm in the United States!"

"Why do you want to see it?"

"Because I'd like to learn about your life and what's it like for a Chinese person to be a student here." Still hesitant, she finally gives in and leads me up two flights of gray cement stairs to a dark hallway that a number of families have turned into a storage area for their gas burners and kitchen utensils. When you live in a single room, space in the hallway for a kitchen is more than welcome.

Apparently this floor is inhabited by teachers and students alike, for further down the hallway I hear a baby cry. Song's room turns out to be a tiny cubicle which she shares with a Japanese student. Contrary to her announcement, it is perfectly clean; she was embarrassed only for its simplicity. The room contains merely two metal cots, each covered with a hard thin mattress and blanket on top, and a couple of trunks at the foot of the bed which serve the multiple purposes of suitcase, storage space for clothing, and table to set dishes on. The bare, dark gray walls, the cement floor and the small window are the primary reason that the room appears like a cell. Song tells me that it is exceptional to have a room like this for only two people. Most students live in groups of eight in rooms twice this size, with four bunk beds.

As soon as I sit down and we begin talking, I forget the starkness of the environment. One of the teachers from next door comes to join us, eager for an opportunity to converse with a native speaker. Song serves us hot juice (a green concentrate diluted with boiled water) in her tin cup. Memories flood back from my childhood when I had a cup like this and when I lived in rooms no bigger than this one. Suddenly I feel at home.

At the end of our visit, according to Chinese rules of hospitality, my host accompanies me down the stairs and out toward the Foreign Experts Building until, knowing that it is time for her supper, I repeatedly assure her there is no need to come further.

Scenes from Student Life

Last night at a party for the foreign faculty I met Mr. Chou (the French teacher who was so rudely kicked out of his living quarters last winter) and one of his students from the French department. Jacques and I were conversing in English when I asked him to introduce me to the two men next to him. Once I realized they couldn't understand English, I immediately switched to French. They were so excited to find someone else to communicate with! Until now, Claudine and Jacques had been the only Westerners they could talk with. Needless to say, I was urged to come see them in the French Department whenever I wanted.

For some reason it had never crossed my mind before that the language barrier must be as big a frustration for the Chinese who want to talk to us as it is for ourselves. To gain an impression of the West other than through media, they have to rely on their language skills. And those studying French here depend entirely on Claudine's and Jacques' interpretation.

My French has become rusty during the last fifteen years, but it won't take me long to revive it. I look forward to conversing with a whole new group of Chinese people.

One half of the Dalian Foreign Language Institute is located further down the hill, close to the bus stop. The buildings there include three cafeterias, a printshop, the library, and dormitories whereas the south campus has the Foreign Experts Building, the French, English, and Japanese departments, an athletic field, housing for teachers, and further dormitories.

A few days ago Lui Hongwei, one of my older students, took me on a tour of the north campus, since I had wanted to see the cafeterias and the library facilities. It was almost 4:30, the beginning of the dinner hour. Clusters of students were playing soccer and basketball in the large yard in front of the building. Ducking to avoid the balls, we made our way through the crowd until we entered the dining hall.

I had been forewarned by the foreign faculty that the environment would be stark, the food unappetizing, and the atmosphere depressing. For the most part I can say that they were right. The hall with its naked walls and cement floor looked dirty in its ugly dark gray color even though it had been freshly washed. Crowds of students gathered around windows on one side of the hall through which food was dished out onto their tin bowls and plates. Along the wall to my right stood several shelves where students could store their dishes after having dumped the leftoves into a barrel and rinsed their plates in cold water in a trough-like sink further back on the right.

Lui Hongwei invited me to take a look through the window. Those in line stepped aside to let me see, even though they probably wondered what on earth I was doing here. The windows opened to another large room with several huge black kettles of steaming hot food. On one side of the hall students could pick up rice (three cents per bowl) and fist-size buns of Chinese steamed dishes with meat and vegetables. To me the quality of the food did not look all that bad. I felt more repelled by the manner in which the food was served and by the containers out of which it had to be eaten. The scene reminded me of old movies of state penitentiaries.

I think if I had come here as a foreign student without any special privileges, I would have purchased more appealing tableware and tried during mealtime deliberately to ignore the environment and concentrate on talking with my classmates. People are creatures of habit. After a while I may have come to laugh at my dependency on fancy dishes. It is amazing what one can learn to get by without!

Walking up the hill to the institute we hear a loud roaring noise from one of the buildings on the right. Angela and I stick our head in and see a group of perhaps sixty students roller-skating on the cement floor of a large hall. Our Tai Chi teacher is there, supervising the class. Several of our English students wave and motion us to come in. Someone rounds up three pair of stakes for the children and me, and before we know it, we have joined in the fun. As we go around the circle, a hand slides into mine. A young Chinese woman and I are skating as a pair, as friends do in China.

Once a year the student from our Institute drive out to a hill south of the city to plant new trees. This time Alicia and I join them. It is one of the first really warm days in early April, ideal for an outing like this. We climb the mountain where groups of students are already busily at work digging holes. They cheer as they see us arrive, genuinely pleased with our interest and our presence. One of them hands me a tiny tree shoot to place into a newly dug hole in the hard, rocky soil. "Have you ever planted a tree before?" she asks. So I tell her about my garden at home, without mentioning the contrast between the moist, rich soil behind our house and the dry, dusty brown earth my fingers are now working with. Will this little tree live? We are told only twenty percent of those planted actually survive. We give the new shoots plenty of water, but in less than a day it will have evaporated.

Our efforts here in China come to mind: a Chinese hand in mine, growing affection between my students and me, moments of deep sharing . . . but in a few months I will be gone. Will the friendship last? Will the memory be strong enough to survive when it is no longer freshly nourished? One can only plant and hope.

If I ever come back to Dalian, I will visit this hill, find a beautiful tree, and claim it is the one I left behind.

Holy Week

"Do you really believe in God?" whispered Sui Aihua next to me as we listened to Susan McLean's lecture on the Bible in Western literature.

"Yes, I do."

Sui looked at me with an expression that said, "How can someone as intelligent as you believe in something that weird?"

"If you like, I'll explain after class," I offered and spent the rest of the hour worrying about how best to condense my faith into a thirty-minute summary. Meanwhile the lecture about angels and devils and souls and immortality and other things that reinforced the audience's impression that the Christian faith was a silly superstition proceeded.

Soon I found myself in the classroom, face to face with six professing atheists ready to laugh at my naivete. Trying not to become defensive, I felt the first thing to do was clarify my understanding of God. It was not fair for them to define what God was and then to deride my beliefs as ridiculous. Anyone can set up a straw-man argument and then proceed to tear it to pieces. To take the wind out of their sails, I said:

"There are many different gods. Some of the most frequently worshiped ones in your society as well as mine are money, or power, or social status, or personal honor, or one's family. Don't tell me those gods don't exist in China. Your god is whatever motivates your actions, the kind of thing you live for, die for, perhaps even kill for. Now, because I am a Christian, I have faith in only one God, the one who has worked throughout history as a force of love, justice, and liberation. All the others are false gods. We call them idols. They lead to death, not life. We should not worship them."

As I had expected, they did not accept my premise that they, too, believed in some sort of god and simply had not defined for themselves what that was. They shifted to another question. "Why does God allow evil to happen? If God exists, why doesn't evil stop?"

"God, out of love, has given us the freedom to choose good or evil. If I forced you to be good, you would have no alternative. But love is only truly love if it is offered voluntarily. So we are free to reject God and be evil, if we want to."

I tried to summarize the biblical vision of a good creation where people were initially one with God and the universe but then misused their freedom and made the wrong choices. I told about the prophets calling people back to obedience, faith, and concern for the poor, and about people's continued rebellion.

Perhaps it was too much to expect that they would understand during this first try. They came back to the absurdity of religious belief like a needle stuck in the groove of a broken record.

They dismissed the thought of a Creator God with Darwin's theory of evolution and were surprised to find that I could easily accept both ideas since one was a faith statement, the other a scientific explanation. Furthermore, they thought prayer was a futile exercise like bringing one's wishes before a fairy godmother.

In a sense, their reluctance to take the Christian faith seriously was simply a security blanket. Anything less would mean questioning what they have been taught from early on. A communist trying to explain the worthiness of that system to a group of United States citizens would likely encounter the same scepticism.

Ken dealt with the question of faith in a less risky way. Instead of beginning with his own beliefs, he asked his class to define their values. In broken English, they explained what they understood by Marxism.

"Whenever we do something, we must consider others."

"We shouldn't be selfish. This is very hard to put into practice, but we must keep trying."

"There should be no exploitation in society."

"We have a vision of a very good life for human beings, a future in which all human needs will be met. The whole world will be united. This is in the distant future, but it will happen."

Ken listed all these basic beliefs on the board as the students suggested them. Then he posed more detailed questions and asked for illustrations.

"What difference does it make whether or not you are a party member here?" he wanted to know.

"If you want to become a party member," they said, "you have to study Marxism and become convinced of it. Those who are already in the party will decide whether you have the ability and quality to join them or not. To be chosen, you have to be active, take leadership, be a good worker and an example to others."

Next week in my classes perhaps I too will start with the basic values of my Chinese students. Then we can discover similarities: our vision of God's Kingdom on earth and theirs of the classless society; our aim to love our neighbor and theirs to serve others; a mutual awareness of falling short of our stated goals.

On Maundy Thursday a group of foreign students and teachers gathered at Susan's to commemorate the Last Supper. We followed the Catholic litany but read the same biblical passages used in our church: the passover account in Exodus, John's description of the footwashing, and Paul's words on communion from the Letter to the Corinthians. For our consecrated drink we used Dalian apple wine poured from a white bottle with a phoenix design; for the bread, a loaf from the downtown bakery. Susan had neatly decorated the communion table with a painting of Christ and the traditional picture of the Last Supper. I went through the celebration with a deep sense of brokenness. Looking at the people around me, I saw differences, discord, distance . . . and yet I was willing to accept my oneness with all of them. Christ's body had been broken too.

Lui Hongwei, Ma Wenshu, and Zhu Hong stop me in the hallway of the English department.

"After you talked to us last week," they tell me, "we had a long conversation in class among ourselves and agreed that some of what you said really made sense. So we have decided to go to the Protestant church with you next Sunday."

"Wonderful! It will be much nicer for me if someone can translate what the pastor is saying. I'd love for you to go with me."

"Our English may not be good enough to translate." I assure them that they will do fine, and we agree to meet at 8:15 in front of the main gate to our Institute.

"We also have some questions to ask you," they continue. "Would you mind coming into our class for a bit?"

Of course I wouldn't mind. I am thrilled with their interest in the Christian faith and eager to explain anything they want to hear about.

"A few days ago in class," they begin, "Miss Susan told us about Holy Week. She described the death of Jesus and got so moved that she was almost crying. We thought it was strange that someone would get so excited about a person who died two thousand years ago!"

"Don't you have heroes you admire very much?" I ask them, trying to help them understand. "I bet you tell stories that mean a lot to you and could move you to tears. How about the movie we saw last month about the juvenile delinquents?"

They all nod. "Tell us why they killed Jesus. We heard *what* happened, by not why. If he was such a good person, why did they crucify him?"

So I talk about the historical situation of Jesus' day, the domination by the Roman Empire, the oppression of the poor, the power of the Sanhedrin, the legalism of the Pharisees, and the revoluntary ambition of the Zealots. I show how Jesus gained a large following and became a threat to the ruling elite; how he sided with the poor; how he differed from the Zealots by rejecting violence; how he exposed the hypocrisy of the Pharisees who worshiped the letter of the law but ignored its spirit, which is love of God and neighbor. I tell them the story of Judas the Zealot who, disillusioned with his master's ways, betrayed him for 20 pieces of silver; and of Peter who denied him out of fear; and of Pilate who sought to wash his hands of the whole affair but nonetheless handed Jesus over to be crucified.

The students listen with fascination. These stories don't sound far-fetched and otherworldly to them because they know of warring political factions, back-stabbing, and betrayal by friends. In their own lifetime, my students have experienced similar incidents during the Cultural Revolution.

I describe the arrest in Gethsemane. When I get to the part where Jesus tells Peter that before the cock crows, Peter will deny him three times, Zhu Hong objects, "But how could he know that ahead of time?"

"Because he is God, you silly," throws in Wei Heping who has attended Susan's lecture on the Trinity.

Knowing that this comment will inject a supernatural element tempting the others again to dismiss the whole story as magic and superstition, I supply a more psychological explanation. "Jesus lived with his disciples day in and day out for several years. He knew them thoroughly. Peter was by nature a passionate, impulsive man who tended to make grandiose proclamations and bite off bigger pieces then he could chew. He promised Jesus that he would be faithful to him even to death. But Jesus knew that at least at this point, Peter was not strong enough to withstand the threat and danger."

The students are with me again, nodding their agreement. "But there is another thing Susan said that we think is weird. She said that after Jesus had died, he came alive again, and that he lives even now. You don't believe that, do you?"

"I believe that Christ is alive in the Church today. The Church is the risen body of Christ."

"The church? You mean that brick building we are going to visit on Sunday?"

"Not the building. The church is not a building; it is the people. We are to continue Christ's works of mercy and teach and live as he did."

"But there are so many different churches. You told us there are fourteen even in your town. Which one is Jesus?"

"There is the wider church of all believing Christians. Within it are many members who form smaller church bodies of their own. Jesus himself said that for him to be present in our midst, it only takes two or three people gathered in his name. In other words, if I meet in a spirit of love with only one or two others ('as with you here,' I silently add), Christ is with us."

A Walk with Cheng

Xiao's friend Cheng takes me on a walk to the east end of the city, where a large number of dock workers live in old one-level brick huts. We walk past the Children's Park with its white swan boats, zigzag bridges, and playgrounds. In the the summer I want to take a boat ride on the lake, if I can learn to bear the putrid smell rising from the polluted water. Cheng points to two stone torches painted red, symbols of children carrying on the revolutionary task. We ask three school girls to have their picture taken with me in front of a child's statue.

We take the trolley to the east edge of town where a new free market has been established that is more fascinating and less crowded than the one beyond Labor Park. Further down is a street with a row of privately run shops: a beauty parlor, a tailor's cottage, and a recently opened bakery. Cheng invites us to take a closer look. First we stick our head into the barber shop, where a man and a woman are just getting their hair done. I see no sinks and wonder how they wash the hair before setting it. Mr. Wang points to a large barrel filled with tap water, a tea kettle humming on top of an old wood-burning stove, and several dishpans to mix the water until it is pleasantly warm. Some day I will come back here and watch the whole process.

Next we stop at the bakery, a tiny room of perhaps ten square meters with a bench for customers on the one side and a flour-covered work table on the other. Immediately on the left toward the front is a display of freshly baked bread, and a round oven filled with a new batch of loaves. The two women attendants are flattered to have foreign guests. They offer us a delicious piece of flaky layered bread and invite us to sit down. We learn via Cheng that it has cost them a thousand yuan ($300) to set up the shop, and they expect to make enough in three months to gain back their investment. "After that," Cheng adds, his voice filled with admiration, "they will make considerably more than the teachers at our Institute whose monthly salary is less than one hundred yuan."

Pleased with our interest in their budding enterprise, the women insist on giving us another bag of scrumptious pastry, "for friendship's sake."

On our way home I notice a gray canvas tent on the sidewalk. "It's for a wedding," Cheng explains. "The tent is used to prepare the food. Would you like to go into the home and meet the couple?"

I hesitate, thinking it might embarrass the wedding party. "I am not sure I should interrupt their family celebration . . ."

"Oh, but I'm sure they would feel honored if you stopped in," Cheng interrupts. "Let me ask for you."

Sure enough, the bridegroom comes out, smiles invitingly, and ushers me in. I find myself in a typical tiny Chinese home with a narrow hallway. A primitive board along the wall holds a dozen plates of delicious-looking salads with seafoods and vegetables. The main room has been transformed into a reception area with the dowry (colorful piles of blankets, pillows, and linen) displayed on the bed.

Excited about the unexpected visit, the bride welcomes us. She looks lovely in her bright red dress and flowers in her hair. With Cheng translating I tell her how beautiful she is and wish the couple many years of happiness together. The bride happily presses dozens of wrapped hard candy into my hand, as is the custom at Chinese weddings. Then the couple want to have pictures taken with me. I am in no way dressed for a wedding, but they don't seem to care. All that matters is the extraordinary chance to welcome a foreigner for this special celebration. So I pose with them and smile while the cameras click. "They will give you copies of the photographs," says Cheng. Everyone is pleased: the wedding party for having had a surprise visit from a foreigner, myself for having experienced still another example of Chinese hospitality.

The Hospital Affair

Xiao came by this morning to tell that his wife, who by now was more than ten days overdue, had been admitted to the hospital. An ultrasound exam had revealed the placenta was old; and so they had decided either to induce labor or to take the baby by Caesarian section. Understandably Xiao was very nervous, although Chinese-fashion, he managed to hide his emotions well. He asked whether Susan and I would like to go to the hospital to pay his wife a visit, and of course I said yes. Xiao realized that, today being Friday, there would be no regular visitation hours; but, anxious about his wife, he figured perhaps the hospital staff would make an exception if he brought foreigners with him.

Susan and I met Xiao shortly after lunch and headed for the hospital. In a passage outside we noticed a blackboard listing recent births: the father's last name, the exact time of delivery, and the sex and weight of the baby. Apparently this served as the waiting room for fathers. Xiao had told me earlier that he would not be able to watch the birth of his son, because up to eight women are in the delivery room at one time. Under these circumstances I doubt that we would let the husbands come in either!

Xiao exchanged a few words with the receptionist at the foot of a dark staircase and indeed received permission to enter. I was impressed. Undoubtedly he had known just what to say to convince her. The process reminded me of the escapade several weeks ago when we got to see the middle school without making prior arrangements. We quickly went upstairs and passed through a series of hallways, all clean but poorly lit and of the usual dusty-gray color that makes Chinese buildings look so depressing. A couple of nurses were wheeling a woman past who had just had her baby. To each side of the hall we could glance into rooms furnished with six to ten cots and filled with patients.

Finally we came to Xiao's wife. Her eyes registered surprise until Xiao explained who we were. When I asked how she felt, she said her contractions were coming two minutes apart. Apparently they had induced labor earlier that morning. A near-empty flask, connected to an intravenous tube, was dangling above her bed. I explained to Xiao that with contractions this close together they would not have to wait long until the birth of the baby. Suddenly a nurse motioned Xiao to come into the hallway. Before we knew it he was back announcing quietly that we had to leave. He bent over his wife, who whispered something in his ear before he joined us in the hallway.

Back on the street Xiao seemed curiously distracted and worried. We got out of him that the doctors had been extemely upset about his finagling to enter the hospital without permissiion. There was fear in his voice. "What's the matter?" we asked. "Surely they won't do anything to hurt your wife or the baby?" Gradually we learned that his wife, with her parting words, had asked him to contact her father, a friend of the head doctor, to plead that they would give her special care. Now, having made the doctors angry, Xiao felt they might not grant the request. Bringing in two foreigners at a time other than visitation hours was already pressing his luck too much.

Susan with her tendency to blame every negative experience on the communists, could't help comment that this was the system's fault. I contradicted her. "If we had gone into an American hospital at a time other than visitation hours, I bet the doctors would have thrown us out too." Comparisons with America are always a red flag for Susan. "But they wouldn't have caused us to be so scared," she objected. Comments like these are for both of us like a lit match next to a gasoline tank. I get furious at her prejudice; she gets furious at my supposed lack of patriotism. This time we both exploded and spent the rest of the walk home in a hot political debate, little aware that poor Xiao, worried for his wife and child, couldn't have cared less about systems of any sort.

Once we got to the Institute, Xiao left to call his father-in-law and then to head back to the hospital to see whether perhaps his baby's name would appear on the blackboard downstairs. I was overcome with guilt feelings. It had been obnoxious of us to fly into a rage about politics at a time when we should have been listening to Xiao's concerns. Moreover, if the doctors indeed refused to give his wife special treatment and something would go wrong at the delivery, I would never know whether we hadn't in some way contributed to the tragedy. Without us, Xiao would never have attempted to get into the hospital at this time. To be sure, he had done it not so much as a favor to us as out of a deep desire to see his wife, whom he knew to be in poor condition. Nonetheless our visit had triggered the series of bad events.

This evening I shared with Xiao's friend Cheng how badly I felt about the whole affair. He assured me the doctors would give Xiao's wife the necessary care. But I know from seeing the overcrowded hospital that "necessary care," which of course must be given to everyone, does not mean much special attention for the individual. It is hard to know whether the conditon of Xiao's wife is indeed serious or whether she is simply going through the same torment every woman would feel if she had to have her first baby all alone in a strange place far from home. I won't feel completely reassured until I hear from Xiao that they have had a healthy baby.

Chinese Hospitality

Mr. He had invited us to his place for dinner. Since he is our teacher of Chinese and has asked his whole class of BCA participants over, the event becomes official enough to make us eligible for a ride in the Institute's minibus.

We are chauffeured to a new housing development on the outskirts of town where He and his wife and son inhabit a tiny two-room apartment.

The boy is about Angela's age, shy and polite, with a butch haircut and his father's round eyes. He's wife welcomes us in Chinese. Today there is no one to translate; we'll just have to practice what we already know. Bob, our star pupil, responds to the greeting with realtive ease. The rest of us stumble through a few sentences and resort to smiles in order to convey that we feel happy to have been invited. He's wife withdraws to the kitchen where she stays, in typical Chinese fashion, throughout the whole meal while we enjoy one delicious dish after another.

Mr. He's brother-in-law, a professional cook, has helped with the meal preparation all day long before we arrive. Never during our stay in China have we received food of such quality, in such abundance, and so exquisitely prepared. A small round card table, set up in the middle of what serves normally as the livingroom, study, and son's bedroom, is the center of the dining area. It carries seven plates smaller than a saucer, placed around a stunning watermelon centerpiece with flowers and designs carved into the rind. We crowd around the table, finding our seats on the bed, a stool, and chairs borrowed from the neighbors. There isn't much elbow space, but the closeness coupled with the simple elegance of the table decoration creates an atmosphere of excitement and expectation. Peggy comments on the careful color coordination: green glasses to matched the carved melon, red dishes to go with the fruit. Chinese cooking, we are told, is to appeal to the sense of sight as well as taste.

Then come the courses—twenty-one in all. Seven are a minimum for honored guests. Fourteen show a high degree of respect; twenty-one are a royal treat. Famished from our long sparse diet of rice and soup, we eagerly do the cooking justice. I can't remember ever having had meat this lean in China. Where did they buy it? What kind of connections did the cook have to procure the ingredients, before adding his masterful touch?

Normally at a formal banquet, the Chinese hosts will serve their guests by piling one helping after another onto their plates. Glasses are refilled after only three or four sips. A "no, thank you" is ignored as nothing but a polite gesture on the part of the guest. An endless battle ensues, with Western guests dutifully gulping down the food until the unending number of courses leaves them completely overwhelmed. After several experiences like this, foreigners begin to develop safety measures. The way to avoid having one's glass refilled is to place one's hand over the top. As for stopping the continuous flow of food that keeps landing on the guest's plate, the only effective method is to eat slowly. An empty plate suggests one is still hungry and thus needs to be served more. What a blow to the Brethren who have always learned to "eat up" what is set before them!

But today we are more fortunate. Foreigners outnumber Chinese, and He, who has grown to expect cultural differences, leaves it up to us to help ourselves. He is delighted to see us relishing the food and gratefully accepts our praise. What a charming host he is! When he smiles, his whole face lights up and wrinkles appear around his eyes. He exudes warmth and happiness that is dimmed only by a sense of insecurity that perhaps he may not please his guests. There is no artificiality in him, no calculation that friendliness will reap rewards. His touching kindness grows from a simple, unpretentious soul.

5

Memories

Bargain Hunting with Alicia

Xiao has a healthy baby boy. He called last night to tell me the good news and relieve me of my worry. For the next few weeks he'll be home taking care of his wife and son.

Alicia and I are making plans for a trip to Shenyang, the capital of our province. One of her students by the name of Lin Tao lives there and has agreed to help us find accommodations and show us around. I am eager to see a place beyond Dalian. It will be easy for us to get away since Alicia can reschedule her classes and I no longer take part in the Chinese language course. Lin Tao has a little girl Angela's age, so we have decided to take Angela along with us.

This morning Alicia and I went bargain-hunting downtown. In a store near Tienjin Street we noticed a pretty display of green and orange glass fish made in the Dalian factory. Since half a dozen fish were left on the shelf and the salesperson was preoccupied with clusters of customers, we decided to shop upstairs first before purchasing a fish on our way out.

It proved a mistake. By the time we got back, all the fish except one had been sold. We pointed to the lovely specimen. "Can we have one like this?"

"Meiyou." No more.

"What about that one?"

"Not for sale." Chinese stores have the aggravating habit of selling everything down to the last piece except one for display to attract the customers' attention. Whoever asks about it gets the frustrating remark that the item is out of stock.

"It drives me crazy," said Alicia. "How can they say they don't have any, when we are looking at one? If they don't want to sell the last one, why don't they just take it off the shelf?"

"We should have bought the fish right away. I thought there were plenty. . . ."

"The rule in China is: When you see something you like, buy it. Don't wait, or it will be gone. I guess we learned our lesson."

Scenes from East Germany came back to mind. I remembered the futile endeavors to shop for specific items. Inevitably they would not be on the shelf that day. It was useless to make a shopping list. The only way to cope was to look at displays and take the chance that something I needed would catch my eye. Often that meant purchasing not what I needed at the time, but something I thought I might need in the near future. In East Germany rarities which, when we were there, included toilet seats, tissue paper, and string, became hot items on the black market. So when a shipment came in, people fell all over the goods, buying them up whether or not they had any use for them. A lucky fellow might end up with four toilet seats. This seemed rather silly until I realized that the seats would turn into bargaining chips to get hold of other material hard to come by. The rule of the game was: If there is a line, join it because something worthwhile is for sale.

In China the situation is similar, only people don't stand in line. Every now and then, in department stores, a long awaited shipment will arrive, causing people to flood to the counter and grab the product. To confuse matters (or is it to diffuse the crowd so that the clerks have space to breathe?), the customer first has to pay for the item at a nearby booth and obtain a sales slip before he or she can trade it in against the precious package.

In a different store near Zhong Shan Square, a supply of desk lamps had arrived. One section of the store had turned into a mob. Fifty hands, held high, frantically waved sales slips while the bodies belonging to the hands pushed and squeezed to get closer to the counter. Occasionally a person would pop out of the mass with the package in hand. On the other side of the store people were opening their packages to examine the lamps they had bought sight unseen. I doubt that any of them had come today with this particular purchase in mind. Yet all who walked off with a lamp before hearing the devastating "Meiyou" left the store with a sense of triumph. They had been in a battle and won.

Memories of Shenyang

Finding a suitable hotel in China is an adventure, especially for two foreign teachers like Alicia and me who don't want to pay tourist fares. From the beginning we had excluded the possibility of staying in luxury rooms for prices similar to those in the United States. Lin Tao took us to a hotel for "Overseas Chinese," but it happened to be in repair. At the next place he was offered a room for sixty yuan (twenty dollrs). Alicia, convinced we could find cheaper accommodation, asked Lin to continue searching. While we sat in the lobby, Lin got busy phoning other places from the manager's office. The manager listened for a while to his fruitless efforts and then said he would give us a special price of forty-two yuan since we were teachers rather than tourists. The Chinese realize that teachers are paid in regular currency and don't have foreign money to throw around. So he had pity on us. Alicia thought the price was still too steep, even at one-third off. Lin kept calling other places. Pretty soon the manager said, "I have another room I can give you for thirty-two yuan a night." That sounded better. We were about to take him up on his offer when he asked about Angela. There were only two beds in the room. Would we need a third one for my daughter? Lin explained truthfully that he had planned to take her home to stay with his own ten-year-old overnight. The manager was aghast. "Don't you know that when you have a foreign guest overnight, you have to register her at the police station?" he asked. Lin said he didn't think keeping a little girl was such a big deal. But the manager, who had meanwhile discovered he had a common acquaintance with Mr. Lin, was deeply concerned for Lin's getting in trouble with the law. He said he would put a third bed in the room at no extra charge. Finally, to top things off, he reduced the price a third time, down to twenty-four yuan (twelve per person, or four dollars, with Angela staying for free).

The room turned out to be beautiful. In addition to the two comfortable beds it had two armchairs, a desk, a color television, and even a private restroom with a shower. One of our three pillows had a hard bean bag stuffing that made a crunchy noise every time I turned my head, until I solved the problem by using just the pillow slip on top of a rolled-up blanket. Overall, the day had been perfect for us. We settled down to watch a three-hour movie on Chinese television while Mr. Lin headed home to his one-room apartment at the outskirts of the city. We learned the next morning that he got caught in a deluge of rain and was forced to spend nearly three hours waiting at the bus stop, freezing and hungry, until the downpour ended and he could walk home the rest of the way.

Early the next morning Lin took us to the Imperial Palace. It was the seat of power for emperor Nurhachi and his son Huangtaiji before the Qing Dynasty established its rule over the whole of China. Most of the pagodas and residence halls, now over 350 years old, have been preserved and beautifully restored in their original design. It was fun to watch clusters of "liberated" Chinese tourists walk freely in "forbidden cities" of former aristocracy, knowing that now these treasures were for everyone to enjoy. We peeked into the emperor's bedroom, the reception hall with the throne, the exquisite homes for the concubines, and the even more luxurious living quarters of the empress. Dozens of little pagodas, each with the characteristic skirted roofs decorated with gold tile, gargoyles, and bright-colored ceilings, had been transformed into museums with relics of a bygone age. They displayed precious dishes and vases, costumes of soldiers and generals, archery items, stagecoach equipment, scrolls and paintbrushes for the emperor, hairpins and brooches for the women, and invaluable tablets with silk embroidery. Outside in the yard amidst marble columns, stone dragons, and incense burners, a school class was having a picnic before continuing the study of their country's rich heritage.

From the palace we took a walk through the old town of Shenyang, where thousands of small brick homes were hidden behind stone walls on each side of narrow alleys. Small children played in the dirt road until we caught their attention. A little boy, too small to work the water pump, ran away frightened as we tried to help him. An area this poor in America would have turned into a rat-infested slum, but here the quarter had remained tidy. There was no garbage in the road, no expression of despair on people's faces, no need to fear an act of violence. Mr. Lin guessed how much we wanted to see one of these homes from the inside. He boldly approached a woman to ask for permission. She turned him down, but an older woman who had overheard the conversation motioned us to follow her. Lin translated for us that she had distant relatives in America and was overjoyed to meet people from the United States.

We wound our way through a maze of alleys to her neighbor who invited us in. Why she didn't take us directly to her own house we will never know; perhaps it was only one tiny room with a bed too small to seat all of us. The neighbor's house had two rooms, one for his parents and one for himself. He had enlivened the stark cement walls with a guitar, gaudy calendar pictures, and photographs of his family, hardly enough decoration to hide his poverty. The old woman's daughter hurried to find two more stools for us to sit on and, once we had sat down, proceeded with typical Chinese hospitality to offer us tea, fruit, and candy. The people were lovely. Images of my own home flashed through my mind. I thought what it would take to be equally generous in our rich setting. Why is it that the poor find it easier to share? I was glad at this moment that the old woman knew nothing of our luxury. As token gifts we left with her a Manchester College pencil and a little Chinese-American friendship pin that we had bought at the palace earlier that day. Before we knew it she had gone to her home and returned with two towels for Alicia and me. After hugs and tears we were sent off with apples, raisins, and our coat pockets full of candy.

Her daughter accompanied us to our next sightseeing spot, the school that Chou En Lai attended as a boy. The building was off the tourist route, so we were the only visitors that morning. Half of the old school complex had been turned into a museum to celebrate the life of the great Chinese leader. We went into the room where he had studied as a child, and I took a picture of Angela sitting at the desk.

Soon it was time for the forty-minute journey by bus to Mr. Lin's house, where his wife and daughter were waiting for us with a delicious seven-course meal. Angela spent the rest of the evening playing with her new friend Lindi. She taught her American hand-clapping games and learned from Lindi how to do a difficult sequence of rope-hopping steps and how to play jacks with rabbit bones. The family urged Angela to stay overnight, but my daughter insisted on going back to the hotel even though she had had a great time with Lindi. Perhaps the thought of being far away from us scared her since there was no possibility to phone and only one person to communicate with in English. Moreover, Mr. Lin lived in a one-room apartment with only one double bed which all four of them would have shared. The bed was a hard, elevated wooden box without a mattress or pillows.

Before heading back we visited with Lin's supervisor who lived in the same apartment complex. Lin led us with a flashlight through pitch-black hallways which some of the families had turned into storage area and make-shift kitchens to enlarge their living space. The boss, a kind man in his late thirties, had an even smaller room than Lin's for himself, his wife, and his nine-year-old son. It contained a set of bunkbeds, a couch, and a desk, at which the son was busy writing Chinese characters. Since living space is assigned and higher positions don't necessarily mean higher pay, it is not unusual that a supervisor will end up with less than the employees below him. During our visit he and Lin were joking about this, apparently without a trace of envy on the older man's part.

Lin wanted to take us clear back to the hotel, but we were adamant that he should not spend another one and a half hours on the road. Alicia had traveled much in China, and we were sure we knew our way back. As it turned out, though, we did get lost. The buildings all looked so different in the dark. Chinese streets are dead in the evening, especially compared to the daytime bustle. We ended up asking four people for directions and meandering around for thirty minutes before we recognized our hotel. If Lin had known, he would have been scared stiff. But he will never hear about it from me.

We spent our second day with Lin and his wife and daughter visiting the tombs to the north and east of the city. These burial grounds for the emperors of the Qing Dynasty are among the biggest attractions of Shenyang, inferior only to the splendid Imperial Palace.

The day started out with complications. To get Lindi out of school, her father had to consult with some officials; so we agreed not to meet until nine. Nine o'clock came, but no Lin. We waited half an hour in front of the hotel, trying to second guess what might have happened. Alicia lost her patience and headed for a nearby department store to shop for souvenirs with Angela. Minutes later, our hosts arrived. The delay had been caused by a power failure.

Since there was no electricity in Lin's area, the trolley busses couldn't run. He and his wife and daughter had to walk for three stations before they could get another bus.

As soon as Alicia and Angela returned, we headed out for the tombs. To our surprise we encountered another stunningly beautiful sequence of pavillions in the same style as the Imperial Palace. We first passed through an exquisitely carved stone gate with eight lion statues and came into an inner courtyard facing a wall brightly enameled with dragons. Three arched doorways opened to a paved road flanked by stone animals and leading to a pagoda that contained an enormous stone turtle, symbol of longevity. Beyond this was a huge square with another ten pagodas encased within thick walls. We climbed a flight of stairs to the top of the wall and looked through the ramparts over the whole complex. At the very end, beyond all the fortifications, was an artificial hill that served as the burial mound. The emperor must have been very scared for his bones and treasures to have erected such an elaborate defense. Mr. Lin told us that ironically even the hill was not the actual grave. The emperor thought it would be too obvious a place. An intruder might dig his body up despite all precautions. So the emperor found another place to be buried, which to this day has remained unknown. To what extent some are driven by their fear of mortality!

As we walked along the ramparts, Mr. Lin told us stories of the emperor. As a young man he was fleeing from an invading army with his baby son. For greater protection he left the child in a tree, located at the bottom of the present huge burial mount, and continued by himself until his horse collapsed underneath him from exhaustion. The pursuing army would have killed him if it had not been for a flock of crows' coming to his rescue. The birds hovered over him and the horse so that the enemy army gained the impression that both he and his horse had been dead for a long time. To the end of his life the emperor fed the crows from his palace to express his gratitude for having been saved.

When he got back to the tree, he found that the branches had closed over the child and the boy was dead. He built the hill as high as it is today because he wanted to have the whole tree covered.

Near the end of his life he consulted a fortune teller about where to erect his tomb. The magician recommended a location at the east of the city where he had seen a dragon and a phoenix fight. According to an old myth this meant that his descendants would continue in power.

If Mr. Lin's stories added to the romance of the North Tomb, the beautiful scenery added to the one in the east. It was located on top of a hill, surrounded by forest. Leading up to the first pagoda were 108 stone steps, a symbolic number reminiscent of 108 outstanding heroes. We arrived at four in the afternoon, only one hour before closing time. Most people had already left, which made the secluded area seem almost deserted—a rare and precious occasion in China. We walked among the pavilions as if they were ours to enjoy alone, as the emperor might have done 350 years ago.

All day Friday we had taken picture after picture to commemorate our visit to the North and East Tombs. Lin had borrowed a camera from a friend and purchased a role of colored film to finish in one day. I noticed that his wife had fallen in love with my coat because she asked me to trade coats with her for some of her family pictures. Happy to have found something she liked, I told her I would be glad to leave the coat in China for her once the weather was warm enough for me to get by without one. Yet the Chinese have difficulties accepting gifts without returning a favor. As much as she loved the coat, she insisted on giving me hers in return. I spent the better part of the return trip trying to argue her out of the trade.

The next morning (wouldn't you have guessed!) Mr. Lin appeared with a package under his arm that contained his wife's coat. I decided to stay firm at all cost and made him carry it home again that evening. When he finally did, I thought I had won the battle. However, once we got back to Dalian on Sunday, he pulled out a gorgeous knitted and embroidered cloth, originally a wedding gift from his wife, that he wanted me to keep as a gift. Again I told him that my leaving the coat did not mean I expected anything in return. In fact, opening his home to us, having us for dinner, and showing us his home town had been such a great gift already. He replied, "You are in China now, so you have to go by the Chinese customs. We want you to have this as a keepsake, and you should take it."

We spent our last day in Shenyang roaming around the city and exploring the less significant sights that were nonetheless fascinating to us. Alicia wanted to see some more sections of the old town. We admired the artful facades of the buildings on the main street. Many elaborate ornaments just beneath the roof had been removed and demolished during the Cultural Revolution. Several layers of paint could not hide the rough, ugly surface underneath the missing design. I wanted to take a picture of the downtown area but found that the crowd was constantly blocking my camera lens. Finally Mr. Lin asked permission for me to climb up to the second story of a large barbershop and take a picture from an upstairs window. Our appearance in the shop caused the usual sensation. I was glad to be back on the road in relative anonymity.

We stopped again at the Imperial Palace in order to have our pictures taken in the traditional costumes of the Qing Dynasty. I was first to get into a red silk robe and try on the heavy headware adorned with jewelry. Part of the outfit was a pair of pretty cloth shoes with awkward two-inch-square soles. In a poor imitation of a gracious princess I carefully stalked over to the cardboard pagoda and posed with a bright smile that must have been totally inappropriate for the period. Then Angela and Alicia took their turns.

We next stopped at a department store, the manager of which was an acquaintance of Mr. Lin from the days of the Cultural Revolution. Back then he was considered a criminal because of his class background and his supposedly bourgeois ideas. He and several others in a similar situation were made to work in a factory as part of a group supervised by Mr. Lin. Whenever other workers wanted to beat the so-called criminals, as was common practice then, Mr. Lin sought to prevent it by saying they needed to be reeducated, not abused. At the end of the Cultural Revolution the man's name was cleared and he was put in charge of what became Shenyang's largest department store with over a thousand employees. Several years ago he visited Mr. Lin to thank him for his kind treatment during the period of difficulty. It would have been nice for us to meet the man, but unfortunately he happened to be in Beijing on business that day. So we went on to visit a museum.

Everywhere people were kind to us and tried to do us special favors. The archivist in Shenyang's large prehistoric museum dug out a huge book with ancient costumes for us to see. The attendant on the third floor served us tea and let us enter a special section of the museum that was closed to the general public because a team of camera men was working on a television documentary. Other employees opened the gift shop for us even though there were no office hours that day. People on the bus offered us their seats. In a public park two men presented Alicia with a big golden candy dragon. Time and again people showed their consideration and good will.

By a streak of luck we ran into Lin's brother in the public park. He had gotten married just a week ago and was taking a walk with his bride. Mr. Lin had expected to see him no sooner than the end of the semester, in mid-July. Of course we were all happy about the coincidence. While Lin visited with his brother and new sister-in-law, we strolled around amidst Chinese couples deeply engaged in serious conversation. Lin explained to us later that young people, after they have been introduced through the arrangements of a go-between, need a place to talk together and find out whether the relationship has potential. So they come to the park to share ideas and feelings. We saw a few couples walking arm in arm, obviously further along in the negotiating process. A decade ago, this close-ness would have been impossible. Lin said that during his days of courting he stayed at least two feet away from his bride until they were married.

On our way back to the hotel I saw my first bicycle traffic jam. Someone had tried to push a bike and cart through a busy intersection near the free market. Within a matter of seconds, with cyclists coming from four sides, the passage became hopelessly clogged. The more people pushed to get out, the worse they got entangled. Since we were on foot, we managed to worm out of the knot and observe the scene from the sidewalk. I couldn't help wondering how they would ever solve the problem. Lin guessed it would take about twenty minutes, but we couldn't stay long enough to see the end.

News and Politics

The international news coverage during the past two weeks has been dominated by the Lybian crisis. Each evening we sit in front of our television set trying to make sense out of scenes showing explosions, victims, and political leaders. Every now and then a Chinese student is with us who can translate part of the commentary, but we usually don't get much more information than we were able to piece together ourselves. Bob listens to "Voice of America" every morning on his short wave radio. From him we obtain a rough idea of what is going on.

Perhaps China is the safest place for an American to be these days. The Chinese news programs seem to suggest that US citizens are targets for terrorists all over the world. Yesterday the chair of the English Department called to advise us not to visit the harbor area for a while, especially the Seamen's Club and the Friendship store. No one is taking his warning too seriously. The Chinese are always overly careful when it comes to protecting foreign guests. Ironically, if someone wanted to hurt Americans here, our own Foreign Experts Building would be a better target than the Seamen's Club.

Compared to the international news, the national coverage has been boring. For weeks now we have been listening to the lengthy deliberations of the People's Congress, which meets once a year during the month of April. There is little debate. The almost 3000 delegates just sit and approve the decisions made by the 133 members of the "Standing Committee." From our China Today class we know that the congress has the power to revise the constitution, to see whether the constitution is justly and fairly carried out, to make and revise laws, to elect the chair and vice chair of the congress, to approve the nomination of the premier and the heads of the state council, to elect the chief justice, to approve the budget and social development plans, to establish special economic regions . . . Night after night we see the leaders in their plain green and blue suits sitting in their stuffed armchairs (the same we have here in our building; there seems to be only one kind in China) next to a table with a cup of tea on top and a spittoon down below. Their simplicity is impressive. I only wish the camera station would blend in other scenes to illustrate what is being talked about.

We asked in class how one becomes a member of the People's Congress. Apparently the delegates are appointed "from above." A special committee decides which percentage is to represent which group or class. At present, over 21 percent are women. 27 percent are workers and peasants, 21 percent cadres ("leaders," administrators), 24 percent intellectuals, 18 percent overseas Chinese or representatives from other parties and organizations, 14 percent minorities, 9 percent PLA. The number of intellectuals is very high now, whereas during the Cultural Revolution the workers and peasants were in the majority. The percentages reflect the current political mood in China. To get the appropriate numbers, the national leadership will tell the provincial governing bodies what kind of representatives are sought, and directives are handed down from there. For instance, the work unit here at the Foreign Language Institute may be asked to supply a candidate who is a woman, an intellectual, and from a minority group. Thus the ballot is structured in order to get the desired representation.

I respect the effort of the Chinese to include women among its leaders. Unlike the US, the equality of women here is a legal right guaranteed in the constitution. Unfortunately, the practice still falls somewhat short of the theory. There is no woman in the Standing Committee of the Polit Bureau of the Communist Party, the most powerful institution in China today. Its members Deng, Li, Chen, Hu, Zhao, and Peng hold key offices such as Chair of the Central Military Commission (Deng), President of the People's Congress (Peng), "Chairman" of China (Li), Premier Minister (Zhao) and General Party Secretary (Hu). Because of the long tradition, the subordination of women is still deeply ingrained in the culture; but since all the women are in the work force and thus financially independent, their self-confidence is rising.

The Chinese government, we learned, also makes an effort to support minorities. Over 93 percent of the population (937 million people) belong to the Han nationality. The rest is made up of 56 different nationalities, all of which are represented in the People's Congress with at least one or two representatives. To protect the minorities and encourage numeric growth, the government has issued special legislation in their favor. For instance, minority families are allowed two children. During periods when the meat was rationed, they were given a better allotment than the rest of the people.

Many of the decisions made by the People's Congress indicate that Mao's ideas are gradually disappearing. To get away from lifetime appointments, the law is now limiting the term of service for the Chairman to only two years. The power of the Congress has been increased. Ownership in the countryside changed with the disappearance of people's communes. Wall posters as a means of public criticism have been outlawed. The representation in Congress is more even and shows less class consciousness.

Every night when we watch the dull scenes with China's old men in their upholstered chairs talking and nodding, I wish I could understand what decisions are being made. China is rapidly changing, and most people think it is for the better. We lack the language skills to hear about the policy changes, but we see the results in the streets of Dalian.

Memories of Yinkou

On April 21, the heat went off, perhaps because the weather had been mild for a while or because this was simply the date designated by the provincial government. It so happened that the very next night Liaoning Province was hit by a storm followed by ice-cold Mongolian winds. The day Alicia, Stefan, and I set out for Yinkou it was drab and drizzly outside. We stayed in our coats the whole time we were on the train. When we arrived at Yinkou, the drizzle had turned into a steady rain. To avoid getting soaked, we stopped at a department store for a while on the way to the hotel.

Zhen Chi, another of Alicia's students, had reserved a room for us on the fourth floor in one of the two hotels open to foreigners. However, upon arrival we learned that the whole fourth floor was occupied by a Chinese delegation to a big conference which was to end that evening. So they first took us to the seventh floor and told us to rest a while. I could not believe the plushness. Even the halls were carpeted. The room with its wide soft beds, fluffy pillows, cozy blankets, and exquisite color coordination compared favorably with a nice Western motel. So it was possible to build places like this in China! Walls without smudge spots and ugly holes; floors where the carpet seams don't show; airtight windows with curtains that slide back without getting stuck; a beautifully tiled bathroom . . . . I thought of Claire's comment that the criterion for appropriate accommodations in China is not "good" but "good enough." What the Chinese students and teachers had in Dalian was good enough for the Chinese, what we had in the Foreign Experts Building was good enough for us, and this hotel room was good enough for those willing to pay seventy yuan per night in foreign currency. Seventy yuan (twenty-three dollars) is not an outrageous price for Westerners. Perhaps foreign tourists always stay in rooms like this one on their China tours.

Our seven dollar room downstairs, when it was finally vacated, proved more than adequate. It even had a Western toilet and bathtub. The floor attendants got so excited about the visit of a blond-haired Western boy that they could hardly keep their eyes and hands off him.

To make good use of our time in Yinkou, we decided to ignore the rain and go for a twenty-minute walk to a nearby Buddhist monastery. We carefully watched our steps, jumping across puddles and balancing along dirt roads that had turned into slimy ridges of mud. The monastery happened to be closed to visitors that day. We peeked at it through a stone fence. The buildings looked dark and gloomy, not only because of the grey sky, but also because Yinkow, unlike a bigger city, does not receive as much money from the government to restore its tourist attractions. Under the pretty skirted roofs and gargoyles the colors had faded.

It was too cold to stay longer. Zhen Chi suggested we have a meal together at the home of his girlfriend Xu Meihua. We thought it would be too inconvenient for them to shop for food in the rain, but they were adamant. Zhen Chi took us back to the hotel to rest while he and his friend prepared the meal. By this time I had gotten thoroughly chilled. We noticed that the outer window in the double pane was broken in several places and that the draft was strong enough to move the curtains. I dreaded the idea of going outside again, but I didn't want to offend our Chinese friends. Around six o'clock we went downstairs to the reception hall to wait for Zhen Chi. Immediately a crowd of Chinese people surrounded us, including the manager, urging us to eat in the dining hall. An English-speaking Japanese guest translated for a Japanese-speaking Chinese attendant that we were invited to eat elsewhere. Concerned we might not find our way, they wanted to know the name of the restaurant. The manager made a gesture indicating it was raining outside. (As if we didn't know!) We were just in the process of explaining our dinner plans when Zhen Chi and his girlfriend showed up, both completely drenched, with rain still dripping down their faces. They were carrying a basket with bottles and food. To our great relief Zhen Chi had decided to save us from having to go out again. He and Xu Meihua had bought some cold dishes for a picnic in the hotel room. We spent the next hour laughing, taking pictures, eating our fill, and making the best of a bad situation. Zhen Chi and Xu Meihua feasted on a bag full of cold prawns. It was fun to watch them crack the shell open with their teeth, suck out the meat, and relish this Chinese delicacy we refused to have anything to do with.

An hour later our friends headed back out into the rain while we crawled into our beds in an attempt to stay warm. I had never been this chilled before. Even with three layers of clothes and underneath two heavy blankets my body refused to generate heat. I finally wrapped a washcloth around the tin water bottle that Jacques had lent us, filled it with boiling water, and put it into my bed to warm my feet. That, and Stefan next to me, did the trick. With our heads propped up with sandbag pillows we watched television for another two hours until a gory Chinese mystery movie about a hotel murder finally put us to sleep.

The next day was overcast again. We had hoped the weather would change, as it had our first day in Shenyang. Because it was so wet, gray, and muddy, we decided to go back to Dalian that same day since it would be impossible to make our way into the countryside. Fortunately the rain had stopped; at least we would be able to visit the downtown area. Zhen Chi picked us up after breakfast and took us to the canal that connects the harbor-city Yinkou with the capital, Shenyang. Was it the gray sky that made the city so drab-looking? The only pretty house fronts were on buildings left from the Japanese occupation. Most homes we saw from our bus window were of the usual red brick or had the dull grayish brown facades of modern Chinese apartment buildings. The canal itself was the color of dirty dishwater. We looked at its polluted surface, surprised that Zhen Chi would find the scenery "beautiful." He told us he often swims across the canal in the summer time. We got the impression that Zhen Chi was sincere in his statements about the beauty of his home town. Perhaps beauty, like wealth, is relative. Maybe some day I can look at scenes like these and admire them too. Dalian, which had struck me as impoverished when we first came to China, already looks luxurious in comparison to other places.

We took the ferry over to a nearby island big enough to have its own village and school. When we arrived, the school children were just getting ready for a big outing. Their teachers were taking them to a movie about juvenile delinquents, the same we had seen in Dalian. (Apparently, once a new film is released here, everyone goes to watch it!) We went past the school to the corner of the village to gain an impression of real Chinese countryside. If life in the country had ever seemed romantic, the slushy mud roads and the tiny unheated shacks quickly destroyed our illusions.

Zhen Chi wanted to be sure we would meet his family before returning to Dalian. Having taken the ferry back to the mainland, we made our way through what surely must have been one of the poorer sections of town. Zhen Chi called it "a funded district," meaning perhaps that by next year some of the roads would be paved. By now we had gotten more adept at avoiding the squishy mud puddles. We couldn't help wondering how Zhen Chi had managed to make it home through these unlit alleys during last night's rain storm. Even more amazingly, the children who were playing outside and the people who stuck their heads out to gaze at us looked remarkably clean. The Chinese must be so tidy, living in conditions like this and keeping as neat as they do!

The brief visit at Zhen Chi's house and that of his girlfriend left but fleeting impressions: a gentle mother scrubbing windows; a parlor with a sofa and radio, decorated for a younger brother to be married a week from now; a brief rest on a hard but smooth wooden box that served as the family bed; a trip to the "outhouse" which was nothing but wooden boards over a squat hole, hidden behind a "curtain" made of bamboo sticks; a father giving his son money to take us out for dinner; and two rich Americans humbled again by the generosity of the poor.

We had to hurry on to the train station. The express train was late, which left us an hour to eat *jiaozi* in a nearby restaurant. The type Zhen Chi ordered was a local specialty. Surrounded with the normal steamed dough, it had a delicious meat and vegetable filling and was open at the top. The waiters brought three piping hot bamboo trays, each with two dozen steaming *jiaozi* shaped like pretty little flowers. After the meal Zhen Chi and Xu Meihua sent us off with a sack of fresh pears and several loaves of our favorite kind of twisted bread, "so we wouldn't get hungry on the way."

Much of our trip to Yinkou will remain in my memory. Years from now, when the brick shades and mud roads have given way to modern districts, I will still remember how it used to be. Leaky tile roofs covered with cheap canvas held in place by bricks, paneless windows covered with plastic sheets, broken boards turned into wood fences—areas of poverty inhabited by people who seem not to know what poverty is, who are happy, excited, curious, and hopeful. Children in youth-league uniforms are playing their care-free games of hopscotch, beautiful and pure like lotus flowers risen from the mud.

A Glimpse of Christianity in China

Several weeks ago when I went to worship at Dalian's Protestant Church, Sui Aihua and Ma Wenshu volunteered to accompany me, curious to find out what a worship service was like. That day a woman preached: Pang Enmei, ordained in 1983. I had brought the two Chinese-English New Testaments we found in our apartment when we moved here. Sui found out from her neighbor that the Scripture for the day was from Corinthians 15. After I had located it, Sui joined in the responsive reading with the rest of the audience. Unfortunately, the passage was on the resurrection, a doctrine very difficult for the Chinese to comprehend. Later in the services I showed Sui the teachings of Christ summarized in Matthew 5-7, which she studied with interest.

The whole way back we talked about religion. Ma told me about her communist ideals of service, sacrifice, and selfless dedication to the common good. Her values were beautiful, very similar to Christian ones, and I didn't hesitate to tell her so.

I had long wanted to talk with the pastor but had needed a good interpreter. Fortunately, Xiao offered to help out by going to church with me last Sunday. After the services one of the elders asked us into an office and served us tea. "We are glad to have you visit us," he said when Xiao had introduced me. I told him I brought greetings from my church back home and was happy to find the faith practiced and growing in China. He proceeded to fill us in with some data about the church here. There are two thousand practicing Protestants in Dalian; five hundred come to the Sunday morning service; the community has four pastors, two male and two female; an additional fifteen hundred believers worship in the area around Dalian. At this time there are around seven million Christians in China.

The preacher, Pang Enmei, a woman in her fifties, joined us for awhile. Not surprisingly, she immediately mentioned the "Three-Self-Movement," either to quelch any attempt I might have to inject foreign teaching or to protect herself from a possible false allegation of having promoted foreign contact. She seemed pleased to hear that I was in favor of an indigenous church in China. All too often in the past they had been hurt by missionaries who did not respect their desire for independence and who undermined the church's safety by taking an antigovernment stance. The pastor related happily that new leadership is emerging in the church. The Dalian community had recently sent four of their members to become theology students at one of China's fourteen seminaries.

Xiao had called to my attention during the service that very few people our age were attending—mainly people in their seventies. I decided to ask the pastor about the missing younger generation. She answered a bit evasively that many of them were working. Xiao had hinted in an earlier conversation that joining a church would be regarded with suspicion, and most people preferred avoiding anything that might cause a social stigma.

It crossed my mind fleetingly how nice it would be to make friends with the pastor. But then I dismissed the thought, knowing I could only harm her. Here we were, having so much in common in terms of our faith and our call to ministry, and yet the only loving thing to do was to stay apart. I hope she sensed my good will as I silently blessed her and her congregation.

After she had left, the elder continued to share with us. He told us how the church had been founded in 1910 by Danish Lutherans; how he had grown up in a Christian home because his father had joined the church in 1916; how in 1959 all the Protestant denominations had united as one body to avoid divisions and splinter groups; how he and other members had suffered during the Cultural Revolution in that they had been forbidden to worship and some had been beaten and imprisoned. "Right now is a good time in China for Christians," he confirmed, "the best we have ever had."

During the service Xiao had asked me why God had not protected the Christians better during the trials of the Cultural Revolution. "God protects us by being with us," I said. "Whenever there is oppression and injustice, God is on the side of those who suffer. And when we crucify the innocent, we crucify God. Love and justice always triumph in the end. That is our faith."

To see whether the elder would explain it in the same way, I had Xiao repeat his question. The elder took a different approach, explaining the persecution in terms of God testing the faith of the believers.

(Later on our way home I asked Xiao, "Would you ever place your son into a perilous situation just to see how he would perform?"

"Definitely not," he said.

"That's why I disagree with the interpretation of the elder. I doubt that God, whom we often describe as a loving father, would deliberately allow us to be tortured in order to test whether our faith holds up.")

The elder shifted the conversation back to my support of the Three-Self-Movement. I explained to him how Brethren mission work had centered on responding to human need, as when the tractor unit was sent to China to help control the floods in Shanxi Province. Christ's love was spread by serving others. We did not want to assume an attitude of superiority but simply treat everyone as a brother or sister in Christ. The aim of each of our missions was to contribute to the growth of an indigenous church. And now my husband and I were here teaching English and learning Chinese as part of a cultural exchange program in which giving and taking were balanced and the gain was mutual.

"You are doing much more than teaching English," said the elder. "You are allowing our cultures to grow closer to each other, and you are promoting international understanding."

"Tell me what message you want me to take back to my church in the United States," I said as I pulled out my pencil and paper.

"Let them know that all Chinese Christians honor God, and that we are now truly free to express our religious beliefs. We hope we can pray for each other as we worship in our different countries. We look forward to exchanging suggestions and ideas and welcome more people to come here so we can learn from each other. May you keep the faith and continue to promote world peace in the name of God."

Foreign Experts' Outing to Lushun

About fifty miles southwest of Dalian, at the very tip of the peninsula, lies a famous site in military history: Lushun, better known to us as Port Arthur. Many Westerners have wanted to see this area, but so far no foreigners have been allowed in, with the exception of one Japenese couple to whom the national government granted special permission last year. According to our

Chinese friends, who all have free access to Lushun, there is absolutely nothing in that place that would warrant the precautions.

Halfway between the center of Dalian and Lushun, about five miles into the restricted area, lies a reservoir with a dam and a lovely little park. This week, for the first time since the 1949 revolution, Westerners were allowed to come at least this far. The municipal government of Dalian arranged for all the foreign teachers in the city to have a picnic in the park and admire the blooming cherry trees.

It had been gloomy and gray for the last three days. Even that morning the sky looked overcast, so that I almost decided to forget about the trip and miss out on the historic occasion. But while we were riding on the bus, the clouds suddenly whisked away and the sun came out with full force. The weather turned out to be glorious.

Our friends had been right. As far as we could tell, there really was nothing worth hiding in this area, nothing that gave even the slightest hint of a military zone. To comply with regulations, our Chinese hosts informed us that it was forbidden to take pictures from our bus window. Too bad; the little villages, terraced hills, billy goats, and donkeys would have been well worth preserving on film. So much for military secrets.

The park was pretty, but nothing grand compared to many I had seen in the West. On the other hand, for Japanese people (and over half of the foreign experts in Dalian are from Japan) April without seeing the cherry trees bloom would be like December without celebrating Christmas. I too admired the thousands of freshly opened blossoms. We had picked an ideal time to come. Two weeks from now all this splendor would be gone.

Stefan and I decided to explore a hamlet with about two dozen stone houses. This was real countryside. None of the villagers had seen Westerners before. They watched us curiously until our smiles and greetings reassured them that we meant no harm. We meandered around gardens, admiring their neat rows of vegetables and healthy-looking onion plants. An old man came balancing two buckets of water that were hanging from a wooden rod across his shoulders. He had drawn the water from a well and now proceeded to water his strawberry plants with a large wooden ladle. He looked happy when we congratulated him on his nicely growing crop. His wife stuck her head out of the door and motioned us to come in.

The country home looked not unlike the apartments we had seen in town, except that it had no running water, electricity, or indoor toilet. The entry way served as storage room and kitchen, and the main room had a hard wooden bed, a couple of stools, and a closet. On the wall hung the typical colorful posters of chubby children and happy couples, as well as a large picture frame with photographs of the family.

The old woman gave us a charming toothless grin and invited us with a gesture to take a seat on the bed. I loved her way of showing hospitality, her pride in her simple home, her attempts to communicate, and her eagerness to make us feel comfortable. At a loss for words, I pointed to my camera, then to her and Stefan and the area outside. She agreed to let me take a picture of her in front of her home, but as soon as I focused the camera, her gentle smile disappeared and she looked deadly serious. It wasn't that she had lost her sense of humor; she simply saw photographs as an important matter and wanted to look dignified. As soon as the camera had clicked, she laughed again.

I racked my brain trying to think of a simple gesture of friendship. Suddenly I remembered that half an hour ago a group of Japanese men had given Stefan several bags of dried fish and a can of beer, none of which we had any use for but couldn't refuse because that would have been impolite. Stefan and I dug out the treats and handed them to the woman who, to our great delight, took them eagerly and nodded her appreciation.

We continued our walk past another row of houses and climbed the hill above the village. Sections had been terraced and turned into gardens. Further up, a young billy goat, tied to a tree, was grazing away at the greenery. We soon reached a high brick wall that surrounded the whole park area to keep out unwanted visitors. Disappointed, we returned to the rest of the group.

The picnic turned out to be a feast. Each person received a huge plate full of cold cuts, chicken breast, and lobster, more meat than we are normally served in a whole month here. After the meal the Japanese, less inhibited than usual because of the good food, the beer, and the cherry blossoms, led us in a circle dance in the center of the park. The Americans and British joined the fun with a demonstration of the "Hokey-Pokey." We all ended up linking arms and swaying rhythmically to favorite international melodies, closing with "Auld Lang Syne." Everyone had a great time. In the future I will associate Lushun with this warm display of international friendship. If only this had always been true of Port Arthur!

6

Many-Splendored Things

Clothing for the Dead

On our way back from town Angela noticed a Chinese sign with an arrow pointing down a narrow passage toward the back yard of a dilapidated home. "What does that say?" Angela asked Xiao who had taken us to the dry cleaner.

"Someone who lives there is selling clothing for the dead."

"Selling what?" I asked, thinking I hadn't heard him correctly.

"Clothing for the dead. Do you want me to ask whether we can come in and have a look?

We were too curious to turn down the offer. Xiao disappeared down the alley and came back a minute later saying we had received permission. We followed him through a cluttered backyard into a typical poor Chinese home. A friendly old man with a bald head, round face, and an incomplete set of decayed yellow teeth bade us welcome. Next to a wall closet lay piles of clothing bundled up neatly in linen cloths. The old man untied one of the bundles for us and showed us a fancy blue jacket with a shiny gold lining.

"This is the outer coat," Xiao translated.

"You mean the dead are dressed in several layers of clothing?" I asked.

"Of course," said the old man. "Three sets of pants, and five layers altogether for the upper part of the body."

"And all this is cremated along with the corpse?"

"Yes."

We looked at some other parts of the outfit. The old man proudly displayed a dainty set of paper shoes, a pretty round hat with a blue satin finish, and two painted cardboard pillows serving as support for the head and feet. A complete set comes with details such as a belt, socks, a handkerchief, and a generous supply of paper money of the kind we have seen burnt on the streets. All this is available for 116 yuan, the equivalent of one and a half months' income.

Why, I asked myself, would people invest that much money just to see it go up in flames? But then I remembered that our funerals are often elaborate beyond belief, and at least as costly. Xiao says that more and more people in China opt for a simpler style. There are less fancy outfits for sale with a "Chou-En-Lai style" jacket, fewer layers, and less of the trimmings. Those who choose the expensive version still retain a belief in an afterlife for which the person has to be equipped with adequate clothing and money. The belief is regarded as superstition, but it seems fairly widespread.

On Sex

A person transplanted into another cultural setting has to become acquainted with all sorts of new behavior patterns. The set of rules on sexual behavior is perhaps the most striking difference.

A North American coming to China notices with surprise how freely people of the same sex interact physically. On the street one frequently observes men walking arm in arm or two young women holding hands. At class outings I have seen men holding each other in an affectionate embrace. At dance parties it is perfectly acceptable for men to dance with men, and women with women. We have on several occasions pointed out to Chinese students that in an American context physical closeness between members of the same sex would be interpreted as a homosexual relationship. Whenever we mention this, the Chinese are shocked. There is such a taboo against homosexuality that the very thought of it seems offensive to them.

Ironically, it is probably the strong taboo that frees them to express their friendship, at least toward members of the same sex. Relationships between men and women are much more obscure. When we first got here, I was impressed how the clear notions of sexual propriety made it easy for students to relate in a purely platonic way to each other without having to play the flirting game that is so pervasive on campuses in the United States. I felt strangely relieved that, since women were off limits for the men, students didn't have to spend their energies trying to define for themselves and others how far to go. It looked like one could be friends with and relate to others with a child-like innocence that I knew was lost in Western society.

Meanwhile I have realized that here, as everywhere, people have to come to terms with their sexual desires. Even here, despite the taboos, limits need to be defined. Only the point at which a relationship shifts from platonic to romantic occurs much sooner. Where we would take a hug or a teasing comment as perfectly harmless, here it might be interpreted as promiscuous. Because of the need to repress one's feelings for members of the opposite sex, which is ultimately impossible, a simple look or a touch of a hand can become a signal between lovers. Emotions are carefully hidden, but that makes the love game even more romantic and, perhaps, more sexual.

How does a touch or a look become sensuous? Where is the line between casualness and intimacy? We all intuitively discern how people feel, and in our own culture we know exactly when and how to draw the line. But here in China the patterns are different, and people are not as easy to read. I had hoped I would not need to be self-conscious. Knowing about their sensitivity, I would not have dreamed of hugging a Chinese man, no matter how good a friend, and so I felt my behavior was irreproachable. But in China the limits are different. Harmless gestures from our viewpoint, such as helping someone up a hill, or taking someone's arm to prevent him or her from being hit by a bicycle, or simply going for a walk as a pair, can take on sexual connotations.

The other day Xiao took me and my children to the Dalian zoo. With great tactfulness he brought up the subject of "limits" in an oblique way. He had read about the high divorce rate in the United States and wanted to know the reasons.

"Is it true that your marriage relationships are more open?" he asked.

"Define what you mean by 'open,' " I said. "Openness" in English is a positive term, and yet I had a suspicion that he in fact was asking about the level of promiscuity in our country. He seemed embarrassed by my directness. To help him out, I volunteered the information. Yes, there was probably a much higher rate of extramarital affairs. But at the same time there were plenty of people who took their marriage vows seriously and who saw adultery as a sin. I made clear that I belonged to the latter group. All at once I was acutely and painfully aware that I had needed to define my position. I couldn't help asking myself whether I had already overstepped the line of propriety, simply by developing a friendship with a Chinese man. And I felt sad that from now on I would have to be more guarded.

First Class to Chengde

I had never in my life travelled with a tour group. Suspicions of long waits, days wasted on attractions I didn't want to see, nagging travel companions, and impenetrable clusters of tourists hovering around a guide like bees in a hive—all these things almost made me not want to go.

As it turned out, the trip to Chengde was a great success. Someone had done a good job of planning. The time at each stop was long enough to see everything at leisure and short enough so that no one became impatient. Visits to Buddhist temples and pagodas alternated with mountain climbing and hikes along the wall around the imperial gardens. At each spot, after a short introduction, we were free to do our own thing until the announced departure time.

Having "roughed it" on hard seats and street food during the trips to Shenyang and Yinkou, I welcomed the experience of traveling as a VIP. Our "soft seat" compartment had more generous leg space and was prettily decorated with white curtains, embroidered table cloths, and shell pictures. Only one person smoked. Instead of dried fish and candy, people sold jade jewelry, medallions, and bamboo fans. The waiters brought not just hot water but also a set of cups and an assortment of bagged tea. Meals were served in the dining compartment.

The overnight train ride from Shenyang to Chengde was spent in a comfortable "soft sleeper" cabin for four. Each time we took a new train, our guides channelled us through to a special first-class reception hall so we would not have to wait in line. Anyone familiar with the cheap way of travelling in China can understand that it was fun to be spoiled for a change. No more people spitting in the aisles; no more thick clouds of smoke; no more squatting over a hole in the soggy and filthy toilet. Our hotel in Chengde, although considered first class, still had bed bugs and lacked hot water; but it was better than others I have seen. And the food on the whole trip, especially that at the two banquets thrown by the province officials in honor of the Foreign Experts, was very good indeed.

It was wise to come to Chengde at this time in Chinese history. A travel guide published just last year in the States said there was nothing much to see because the vandalism during the Cultural Revolution had turned most of the temples into ruins. This comment was based on a 1983 visit. In the last three years a remarkable effort must have been made at restoring the many sights to their original beauty. Even as we were visiting the temples, people were repainting ceilings and picture frames. Many halls that are now empty or used for storing equipment for the restoration process will soon be turned into museums to display ancient relics and costumes. Five of the eight Buddhist monasteries have reemerged in their majestic splendor. In another three years perhaps Chengde will be flooded with Western tourists, like the well-trodden paths around the Ming Tombs.

My birthday fell on our last day in Chengde. Early that morning we climbed a mountain with a huge carrot-shaped, eighty-meter rock at its peak. The path wound its way over sandy hills and along steep cliffs. At times the drop on one side was so drastic that I was gripped by the dreadful thought of slipping and breaking my neck on the rocks below. The rolling hills of Northern China are almost void of trees. They look like an endless brown sea, rather desolate if it weren't for some terraced gardens planted even at this high altitude. Because of the lack of vegetation, we had a splendid view from every point along our path. The last stretch was so steep that we couldn't have proceeded if it hadn't been for stone steps leading up to the top. At one point I made the mistake to look back. I wished I could have turned into stone, like Lot's wife, to avoid having to make my way back down those stairs. Going up was all right, going down was not. I got dizzy and sank down on all fours, hanging on to the stairs for dear life. Why on earth had I been dumb enough to climb up here? About forty feet above, some of our group were resting on a plateau next to the enormous rock. Gradually, a step at a time, I moved to the top myself, only to find that the plateau, which I had imagined to be vast, was the size of a small room, with absolutely no walls or rails on any side. I crept toward the middle and sat down, petrified with fear, unwilling to budge a single inch. The terror inside me released itself in a flood of tears. Again I asked myself how I could have been stupid enough to try this. For some reason Bob, Angela, and Ken were moving around freely, taking pictures and looking in all directions, as if the thought of tumbling down that cliff didn't matter at all.

Needless to say, I did get back down. With Ken and Bob in front of me, my hands dug into their shoulders, my eyes firmly focused on their heels, I took a step at a time and pretended to forget where I was. By the time I arrived at the temple I was ready to ponder Bob's comment that soon I would look back on this event and think it had been a lot of fun.

Word got around about my birthday. During lunch our group sang the traditional "Happy Birthday" song for me, and the Chinese cooks brought out a dish full of noodles. (Why noodles?) On the train to Beijing that afternoon Bob pulled out three packages of round flaky cookies to serve as a substitute for cake. For some reason the train was held up repeatedly on the way, causing a four-hour delay. Shortly before midnight we reached Beijing, where my birthday ended with a huge banquet in the Friendship Hotel.

Love: A Many-Splendored Thing?

To celebrate the birth of his baby boy, Xiao asked Alicia and me to come over for a meal with his family. After dinner the discussion shifted to the topic of love. "What kind of qualities are you looking for in your partner?" I asked Xiao's younger brother who was of the proper marriage age and had a girlfriend he was likely to marry within a year.

"She should have a good position and be beautiful, intelligent, and motherly," came the quick reply. It seems the Chinese think about this question a lot, because they have their answers ready. Sometimes the specifications are precise enough to include body height and eyelid shape. (In China, the "double eyelid" is a sign of beauty. Less than half the population have this much-desired groove about the eye.)

"If you can specify exactly what you are looking for, then what role does love play?" I asked.

"We don't pay much attention to love," said Xiao, grinning at my romantic streak. "In the West, you probably are just as calculating in your choice of partners. You just don't admit it."

Of course I denied that this was true. Specifications about body size and facial features would turn the propective partner into an object like beef examined at the county fair.

I thought it was crass. I also didn't like the idea of having a child with a person I didn't love. Xiao argued there was nothing wrong with it, and we went back and fourth, in part because we really disagreed and in part because we enjoyed the debate.

Claire told me the other day she had heard from a Chinese friend that most women have romantic attachment to a man before they get married to someone else. Shortly before their wedding, they go and confess their undying affection to the man they love. Then they carry their feelings in their hearts for the rest of their lives while building a marriage relationship for the sake of convenience and social expectations.

Sometimes the pattern is different. Cheng confided yesterday that a good friend had asked him for advice concerning his budding relationship with a classmate. He and the girl had fallen in love with each other, but when the girl told her mother about her feelings, the mother disapproved. With college graduation another two years away, she was expected to dedicate herself full-time to her studies rather than think about men. Moreover, the friend was from the countryside, so the mother thought her daughter could make a better catch. For over two weeks the couple waited, undecided about what to do. Then the girl's brother came for a visit to confirm the parents' opposition to the match.

Cheng wanted to hear from me what I would advise under the circumstance. When I suggested trying to persuade the parents by recommending the boy to them, he said they would interpret this as his endorsement of the relationship and hold him responsible for having encouraged the romance. I suppose in an American setting my suggestion would have been that since both students were of age, they had a right to choose their own partner. However, this was China. Going against one's parents' wishes and severing the relationship with them would be an extremely heavy burden to put on a young marriage. The couple would lose financial support and be frowned upon because of disrespect for the older generation. Obedience and love for one's parents are still values much stressed in China. So Cheng felt, and I agreed with him, that terminating the relationship would probably be the least painful in the long run.

War of Independence

Our Chinese students continue to be amazed at our ability to find our way around in Chinese society. They talk about some of the sights of Dalian and are surprised to find that we have already been there. Or they meet us some place and are afraid we may not find our way back to the Institute. They marvel that we manage to use the bus system and buy what we want at the free market or in the department stores downtown.

Yesterday, when Xiao was particularly obnoxious about my needing his help to get around Dalian, I accused him of male chauvinism. He was amused to find that the concept existed even in the West and didn't seem a bit insulted. He argued Chinese society had come a long way since feudal times when women were the mere property of their husbands. Then he decided to flaunt his chauvinism by proving to me that I indeed couldn't get along in China by myself. The next time we entered a store, he said, "All right, you're on your own. Go ahead. I won't translate. You said you could do it." Of course it happened to be a store with a particularly uncooperative staff. I pointed to the object I wanted, but the woman behind the counter only looked at me with a blank stare. Xiao observed me gleefully as I tried again. Finally, when the storekeeper personally asked him to translate, he condescended to enter the discussion.

I was furious. Mustering all my self-control, I put on an expressionless mask to hide my anger. If I had been by myself, I would never have attempted to purchase something in that store. I would have simply given up and gone away without feeling humiliated. Stupidly enough, for the whole rest of the walk I kept demonstrating to Xiao that I could indeed fend for myself. I got across to the ice cream vendor that I wanted vanilla instead of chocolate; I bought a pound of peanuts and rejected some baked goods because they were too expensive; and I found the way home with no problem. It was a childish desire to prove my point after I had already lost the argument.

Only the next afternoon did I realize fully what had hurt me so deeply. I was on my way to the Dalian Technical Institute to give a presentation on the Christian faith for one of Claire's classes when I suddenly remembered that I had not counted the number of bus stops. How would I know where to get off? Xiao had told me that everyone in Dalian would understand "Dagong," the abbreviation for the school; but when I tried it on the conductor, she didn't have the slightest idea what I meant. I was overcome with a feeling of helplessness. Why was it no one could understand English? Why did my bits of Chinese never make sense to the local population? The debate with Xiao came back to mind, along with the painful awareness that he was right. I could not fend for myself. This time I hadn't even needed him to prove it to me.

Somehow I accidentally got off at the right place after all. It struck me that two different issues had become confused in my mind. One was that of alleged female dependence on a man who would straighten out problems for her. The attitude that women were somehow less well equipped to cope with life was indeed revolting. But my own dependence had a different cause, unrelated to the sex issue. For the first time in my life, I was in a country where people spoke a language I didn't understand, and recourse to Spanish, French, German, Dutch, or English didn't do a bit of good. I was dependent on Xiao not because he was a man, but because he spoke Chinese. He had taken me places I would have never discovered and had interpreted customs and behavior patterns that would otherwise not have made sense. I knew I owed him a lot. Nonetheless it was unfair for him to make that point himself by letting me feel my dependence.

Xiao called that evening to tell me he believed women could do "everything." I had to laugh because he sounded so serious. Then I told him why his behavior had offended me. I think he understood.

7

Travel

A Boat Trip to Yantai

The children and I had dreamt of an excursion to Yantai for quite a while. Having read another foreign teacher's detailed account of how to get there, I felt at ease about venturing the trip on my own. It would involve spending a night on a boat while crossing the Yellow Sea from the Liaoning peninsula to the mainland; then taking a bus to Penglai, a tourist spot on the coast about two hours away from the city, and spending the day sightseeing; and finally taking the boat back the same evening to arrive in Dalian the next morning.

Since Ken was concerned about our going without a Chinese interpreter, I asked Zhu Hong to accompany us. She excitedly agreed, happy about the opportunity to get to travel and to practice her English for a whole day. We arranged to meet the next morning to buy tickets. At the appointed time Xiao and I waited for her at the front gate of the Institute, but she didn't come. Instead, a friend of hers arrived to tell us she was sick and would not be able to go. It was a bit strange to come down with a sudden illness like that, but I knew enough not to press the issue. Going with a foreigner, I remembered from the trip with Cheng, meant taking full responsibility for whatever bad thing might happen, and being severely criticized if things didn't work out.

Xiao and I brainstormed what to do next. I was quite willing to forget about the trip; but he suggested trying to find another student.

he advised against asking someone from the college-age group on campus because for them to take a day off would require special permission from the dean and might lead to additional complications.

Because of his experiences during the Cultural Revolution, Xiao is always leery of broadcasting one's intentions; getting the authorities involved means asking for trouble. This time his apprehensions seemed unfounded. I learned the following evening when we were having dinner with the dean and his wife, that the students frequently take the trip to Yantai and need no permission to leave on the weekend. On the other hand, perhaps taking a foreigner would have been a different matter. I am beginning to learn, like Xiao, that to ask too many questions is to get too many answers, and that even the authorities sometimes prefer *not* to know so that they cannot be held responsible for having agreed to a risky venture.

Xiao suggested asking Song Zhihui who as an older student might be less intimidated by the administration. More level-headed then Zhu, we found her reluctant at first. She felt her English wasn't good enough. Unsure whether this was just the typical polite gesture of playing down one's language skills or rather a way to tell me she didn't want to risk going, I pressed her for more reasons. But Song insisted the language matter was her only hesitation. I assured her that her English was excellent; and besides, we needed someone with us who spoke Chinese, not English, in order to "make arrangements" for us. Whatever it was that convinced her, she finally said yes. Once she had made the decision, I could tell she too was excited about the prospect of a boat ride.

Finding someone to accompany me had been the first hurdle; buying tickets proved to be another. The day before, Zhu and I had walked to the harbor to check out the prices. It looked like we had a choice of five classes. The first and second one, at over seventeen yuan (six dollars) prohibitively expensive for many Chinese travellers, was for double occupancy. Third class meant sharing a room with six to eight passengers and sleeping on a cot. At nine yuan, this seemed the most desirable option. Going fourth or fifth class (for seven or five yuan) meant just to be on the boat and to sleep on the floor wherever one could find room.

The next day Xiao, Song, and I headed for the harbor to book the voyage. We assumed we had to do so a day in advance, as was true for train rides if one wanted to be sure to get a seat. But when Xiao finally got to the window after having waited in line for half an hour, he was told the tickets had to be purchased the very day of the trip. On our way back to the Institute, we asked Xiao to try again the next morning. He agreed without blinking an eye, but I knew it would be difficult for him. People line up as early as 5 a.m. in cues stretching way out into the street. By eight, all the good tickets tend to be sold.

The next day around 9 a.m. the phone range at my home. It was Xiao, asking me to join him at the harbor as quickly as possible. I rushed down the hill to the bus stop, only to find that the bus had broken down right there. It took twenty minutes for the next one to come. At the harbor Xiao told me he had come before seven that morning, but learned (after a one-hour waiting period) that already the 8 p.m. boat to Yantai was booked solid. Since it was Saturday, another boat would leave at 9 p.m.; but it was a big ocean liner with only second or fifth class tickets at nineteen or seven yuan, and so he was unsure which ones I wanted him to buy. With some exasperation he related how he had been sent to another building to cue up for the next boat. He finally called, unable to decide what to do.

I probably should have been there with him from the beginning. Nothing in China is easy to arrange, and getting tickets to any-where is the worst of all hassles. At least with me present Xiao could have practiced his English, and I could have cheered him up. I taught him a new saying: "Roll with the punches." That's what one has to learn to do here.

We trudged back to the second building, where in the mean-time the ticket counter had been locked shut. Xiao tracked down some officials who told him that, once the line had shrunk to a manageable size, they had moved the ticket sale back to the original place. I couldn't help chuckling as we returned once more to where we had just come from. Xiao, having already wasted three hours, had more trouble seeing the humor in the situation.

Luckily for us, the line was shorter this time. The presence of a foreigner, namely me, did its magic trick. Some officials "adopted us," went up to the window, and procured the tickets—two second class for Song and me, and two fifth class for the children. This way we would have private accommodations and could sim-ply tuck the children in with us.

At sunset Ken accompanied us to the harbor to see us off. In the long tunnel-shaped building before the gate, people were napping along the walls, their heads resting against a sack with their belongings. Song guessed they were probably waiting for a boat to Shanghai the next day. We made our way to the biggest ship in the Dalian harbor, a beautiful white ocean liner with eight life boats and five decks. After the steward had helped us locate our cabin, we went to the railing to watch the lights of the city while the ship gracefully glided out of the harbor.

It was difficult to get to sleep, even though the cabin was comfortable. The steady puttering sound of the motor joined the Chinese dance music and gradually lulled us into an almost trance-like state of relaxation. At 3:30 a.m. the steward unlocked the door and rudely turned the lights on. We had landed at Yantai. If I had ever had any doubt about needing a Chinese interpreter, I now realized the advantage of having Song with us. She negotiated with the steward and received permission for us to remain on the ship until morning. With all the other people gone, we fell into a deep slumber until seven.

Song's presence continued to be invaluable. She booked a cabin for the return trip that night, found the terminal for the bus to Penglai, got us to our destination without problems, found a reasonably priced restaurant, negotiated successfully with officials who wanted to charge foreign tourist prices, asked for directions, and made sure we saw all there was to see. I just relaxed and enjoyed it.

Yantai was a small enough town for us to attract even more attention than usual. A man on the bus to Penglai engaged in a conversation with Angela and Stefan, saying this was the first time he had ever spoken to a foreigner. We did not see a single Westerner the whole day.

Penglai turned out to be a delightful little tourist trap. It was more or less just a stretch of beach with steep natural rocks similar to the ones in Dalian, but the town had pepped up the scenery by putting a fortress and half a dozen pagodas on top of the cliffs. On certain days the mist rising from the sea enveloped the rocks until the fortress appeared like a castle in the clouds. Beautiful from a distance, the buildings lost much of their charm upon close examination. Built in 1981, the temples contained brightly painted monsters and a design that was meant to be traditional but came across as fake.

The place was flooded with tourists. After having squeezed through crowds for half an hour, we fled to the beach, climbed the rocks, and enjoyed the pretty buildings from afar. Angela and Stefan begged for a ride on a ferry boat, again gaudily painted in yellow and green and appropriately fixed up with a skirted roof, dragons, and monsters. We embarked on a half-hour boat ride, admiring Penglai's shoreline while bouncing on the ocean waves.

By noon it had become very warm. All along the shore vendors were selling ice cream and carbonated soft drinks, which didn't do much to quench our thirst but at least kept us from dehydrating. Many other entrepreneurs had found their niche in the budding tourist market. Booth after booth offered an array of local crafts: paper dolls dancing on a stick, shells decorated with scenes of Penglai, polished stones with pictures of the "Eight Immortals," gourds in all sizes with Chinese characters and pavilions painted on them. On the beach a dozen photgraphers had set up bright cardboard stands with headless people in Qing Dynasty costume. For a small fee, tourists received permission to stick their heads into the cardboard for a typical "Chinese picture" pose.

Early in the afternoon we took the bus back to Yantai. We visited a historical museum with five-thousand-year-old pottery excavated near there and a hall with pictures of local revolutionaries from the time of the Liberation. We climbed a hill to a small restaurant overlooking the sea, where we ate a generous helping of *jiaozis* at the grand total prize of 2.20 yuan (70 cents) for the four of us. And we explored the rocky beach of Yantai until it was time to return to the boat.

On the big square in front of the harbor, a bare-chested Kung Fu expert was demonstrating his skill. We joined a group of about a hundred spectators who had circled around him to watch the show. A little boy assisted by beating vigorously on a tin gong to create excitement and attract a larger audience. The man announced his stunts in a Southern dialect unfamiliar to Song, but his gestures spoke for themselves. He threw himself into the typical Kung Fu poses while shouting and hissing to intimidate his imaginary opponent. We watched him break a metal wire wrapped tightly around his arm muscle and smash a couple of bricks with his bare hands. It was an entertaining end to an altogether exciting day.

The second night on the ship passed much like the first. We watched the shore lights disappear in the distance, settled down to rest in our pleasant little cabin, and negotiated again to sleep late into the next morning.

A Beach Outing with the Students

Spring has finally arrived. Bright yellow ginger bushes, fruit tree blossoms, and tiny green buds on the grotesquely trimmed tree branches are sprinkling color over the brownish gray desolation of Dalian's residential areas. My eyes long for the rich, deep green of Indiana's lawns. Grass is not wanted here. Superstition has it that grass breeds insects, so people prefer living with the dust that the wind whips up from the parched earth.

"Let's go to the beach this weekend," Wei Heping and Song Zhihui suggested after class on Friday. "We'll invite a few of our classmates to come with us. We'll have a picnic at Swallow's Nest Island, all right?"

"Fine. What do you want me to bring?"

"Oh, nothing. We'll pick up some cans of food and *qishui*. You just come with your children."

The next day the sky shone in a brilliant blue without a single cloud. We climbed into a bus which, to everyone's surprise, was "empty" enough for half the group to find a seat. I went to the teller to pay the fare for the children and me. When I rejoined the others, I noticed them exchanging knowing looks and suppressing a grin.

"What's the matter?" I asked.

They hesitated, then decided to be open. "We know you well enough to tell you. We are your friends. If a Chinese had done what you just did, it would have been incredibly rude. But you are a foreigner, so we realize you didn't mean it."

"What on earth did I do?"

"You paid just for yourself and your children, even though we had come as a group. In China, one person pays for all. The other way is considered individualistic, looking out only for yourself."

"Oh, really? I am sorry. Here, let me get the other tickets."

"No, that's fine. We just wanted to tell you because you are always so interested in differences between our cultures."

"I guess in America we think it's most fair if we each take care of ourselves."

"Right. That's what we've heard." A little amused smile hovers on Wei's face.

I make another attempt at self-defense. "How do you determine which person pays? Isn't it too much of a burden for one to be stuck with the whole bill?"

"Someone always volunteers. Gradually, each person gets a turn; it evens out somehow. I guess it is an opportunity to be generous. People like it."

The practice triggers so many reflections in my mind. Men pay for women, wanting to be cavaliers but forcing women into dependency. Business associates offer favors, but seldom without strings attached. How is the intricate Chinese system of social grace connected to the maze of back-door politics? When is generosity pure, and when does it become a means to an end? Perhaps some of America's individualistic self-sufficiency is rooted in fear of being set up for future exploitation. China, as a nation, has learned this bitter lesson. She will no longer accept enticing deals that put her solely on the receiving end. On that level at least, the Chinese have understood how crucial it is to take care of their own needs, to "pay their own fare."

As I sat brooding, my friends began to worry that they had indeed hurt my feelings, until I reassured them this was not the case.

We decided to have our picnic at the shore of Fu's Village before taking the thirty-minute walk to Swallow's Nest Island. That way we would have to carry fewer food supplies. Zhao Aiguo found a fairly secluded spot with a clean, flat boulder to use as a table. As soon as we had settled down, everyone started chatting and laughing and clamoring like a typical Chinese dinner party among friends who are having a good time. Lui Hongwei pried open a few cans of beef and fish while Zhao broke chucks off a loaf of bread and passed it around. It was a feast of the poor, in the simplest of circumstances, yet celebrated with great joy. Wasn't this more relaxing than a multicourse banquet that required a stiff etiquette? What elaborate dinner setting could be more impressive than the wide ocean with its foamy waves crashing against the rocks?

"I can't finish my *qishui,*" said Song, sighing contentedly but wondering what to do with her half-empty bottle.

"I'll drink it, if you like."

Song looked at me with a doubtful expression. "But I have already drunk from it," she said apologetically.

"That's all right, I don't mind." I took two hearty sips while she gave a little screech of delight, clapped her hands, and embraced me with a big hug as soon as I had finished.

"Now I know you are really my friend," she said, beaming at me. How did I deserve this affectionate outburst? I smiled back, happy to please her and to have unwittingly done just the right thing.

On the way to Swallow's Nest Island I walked with Zhao Aiguo while Angela and Stefan ran ahead with Lui and Song. Zhao is one of Ken's students, a member of the drill team that gets him ready for his Chinese exams. He is quiet and a bit withdrawn, but always very polite and helpful. I relished the opportunity to get to know him better. He confided that he loves the sea. He comes to the beach every weekend, finds a solitary spot and looks at the ocean waves. It's his time alone, away from the crowds and his roommates and the school.

His need to be by himself did not surprise me. Although most Chinese are very group-oriented, they also have a deep desire for privacy. I remembered the students I had seen walking on the athletic field at dawn; some were engrossed in their books, others studied martial arts. They did not shout greetings or seek to communicate. In the very presence of others, they retained the right to be alone. Others, like Xiao, met their need for privacy by withdrawing mentally and emotionally into chambers of their soul where no one else was allowed to enter.

Swallows Nest Island is a beautiful scenic spot south of Dalian, several miles away from the next bus stop and therefore not overrun by tourists. As we climbed down the steep stairway to the rocky peninsula, we were surprised to find a *waiguoren* coming toward us. I laughed inwardly as I realized how my reaction to foreigners had become more and more like that of the Chinese. They were so noticeable, so different, such a rarity to behold! The man turned out to be an Irish sea captain whose ocean liner had arrived just the night before.

"How do I get to Tiger Beach?" he asked us. We explained that to walk was about the only option from here. Of course there was a bus connection from downtown.

"I have a car to take me there," he said. "We are in Dalian for only one day, so I decided to rent a car. That way we get to see whatever is worth seeing. The driver brought me here."

"How much does it cost to rent a car?" Our students could not suppress their curiosity.

"Sixty yuan a day."

That was about twenty dollars—a bargain price by Western standards, especially since the car came with a driver. Zhao and Lui looked at each other, their eyes speaking volumes. No one said anything. Sixty yuan was about what they had to live on for a whole month. Like our students, we had come to think of money in Chinese terms: three cents for a bowl of rice; eight cents for two vegetable rolls, which made a decent substitute for lunch in our cafeteria; three to five cents for a bus ride. Sixty yuan was an outrageous sum to throw away for a one-day pleasure trip, but this was a Westerner. Westerners had other standards, other lifestyles.

Again I felt set apart, identifying simultaneously with two different viewpoints. The man had done the only sensible thing. On foot he would get to one or two sights at most, and without a guide he would not likely find them. He wanted to see some of China while he had the chance. Who could blame him?

But in my heart I hurt for the Chinese. I felt the economic injustice implicit in some people being able to buy whatever they like. I sensed the vanity and futility of wanting to "see China" in a day, of looking at scenery and being so terribly removed from those who live here.

Later, on the beach, Lui, Zhao, and Yang donned Western-style shirts, pulled silk ties from their pockets, and had their picture taken. They shot a whole role of film because, as Yang explained, Chinese film has to be used up fast or the quality will deteriorate. Where they found the ties I don't know. They probably borrowed them from friends just for this purpose. I thought of Chinese brides who dress up in long, white gowns owned by the photography studio. Once their picture is taken, they change back into the traditional red Chinese wedding dress. It is always the Western way that is most fashionable, most admired—from eye shape and white skin to wedding gowns, suits, and ties. My mood changed from grief to anger and back to a profound sadness about people who could not accept their own beauty.

The Returnee

"See the man over there with the white hair?"

My eyes follow the direction in which Claire is pointing with her head. Sure enough, one person standing next to a group of four faculty members has a thick shock of white hair surrounding his head like a halo.

"What about him?"

"That's Mr. Shu. He emigrated to the United States in the early sixties but returned for good a few years ago. He's an interesting character. You should try to get to know him!"

"I wonder what makes a person want to come back. It seems like everyone jumps at the chance to leave!"

Claire doesn't respond. We walk past the group and continue our walk in silence. Claire has lived here for almost two years, long enough to make it her home. There is still much in Chinese society that gets under her skin, but even more that she has grown attached to. What would it be like, for a man such as Shu, to leave China? Perhaps he felt like a tree transplanted into a soil that lacks essential nutrients for survival. What may he have missed? The lazy comfort of a routine job without pressure; friends to chat and play cards with; thick crowds of people who look and talk like him and who understand his complaints and his laughter; bits of food stir-fried in a wok . . . the sound and smell of home, no matter how simple or even how offensive at times. Home. What is it that makes us want to go back? It is not a rational decision about which lifestyle we prefer. It is more earthly, instinctive—a return to a childhood atmosphere we did not choose for ourselves but accepted as given, like a second skin. The memory of home stays with us wherever we go, warmly embracing and protective, like a womb.

On Repetition

Claudine was beside herself with anger. "You wouldn't believe how many times I have told my students not to plagiarize on their research papers. Again in this last set are five cases where students copied word for word from magazines. I can't believe how easy it is for them to steal someone else's ideas!"

I didn't say anything. It is useless to argue with Claudine when she is in this kind of mood. Besides, I don't appreciate plagiarism either. But I think the concept of "stealing ideas" is as foreign to Chinese people as "owning the land" was for Native Americans when the white people first claimed American territory. Thoughts, once shared, are no longer the property of the one who gave them utterance.

Perhaps the basic cultural difference is that in the West we value originality while China places more emphasis on perfection. Thus a good thought, if borrowed, will improve the mind of the borrower. Analogously, an artist will learn the craft through years and years of imitating famous painters. The motif is given. Chinese pictographs, for instance, don't need to be reinvented. The difference between the expert and the beginner lies in the mastery of the brush stroke. Cao Shengli told me it takes him less than an hour to paint his "Four Seasons" watercolor sequence; but he has put years into practicing. Imitation is not theft. It is a method to study and learn from the masters.

Repetition pervades Chinese life. Universally, children learn by imitating their parents and older siblings; but where a Western child beyond a certain age will soon be criticized for being a "copycat," the Chinese keep polishing their skills by emulating those who do better. The game Angela's school friends play every afternoon consists of jumping over an elastic band in a series of carefully specified steps that need to be memorized. Any originality that would ignore the predefined pattern is perceived as wrong, unless the group together agrees on a more complex sequence.

In a similar way the dances performed by nursery school youngsters are learnable routines. Group harmony counts, not individuality. Young people like classical ballroom dances with a defined sequence of steps. Tango, waltz, and quickstep are popular among our students. Our jerky modern rock dancing, wild and aimless and unrestrainedly individualistic, to them seems a rather pointless exercise until a pattern evolves that is teachable.

It amazes me sometimes that the Cultural Revolution broke out amidst a people so eager to conform. How could a people so obedient and so dependent on cultural norms get carried away with revolutionary fervor and fanaticism? How could the deification of one man drive them to throw away their traditions? Maybe the radicalism of that period had again to do with conformity. Students became red guards because all their friends did. People went along with the witch-hunt for rightists because everyone else did. Perhaps there comes a point where obedient, community-oriented people are easier to mislead then rugged individualists who have to be convinced one at a time.

Getting in Shape, Western Style

For the past three weeks, ever since it got warm outside, Claire has been obsessed with the idea of getting in shape for summer. Walking up the hills around the Institute and climbing eight flights of stairs to our apartments several times a day has toned our muscles, but Claire wants to lose weight. So I have joined her in a long bike trip to the beach as well as for daily exercise sessions. It seems hilarious to me to listen to Jane Fonda's tape ("Stretch it out, two, three, four . . . to your left, two, three, four . . . one more time . . .") and bend and lift until our muscles ache. What a way to import Western habits!

"You should see the wives of businessmen in Beijing," Claire said with a twinkle in her eyes. "They are all fanatic about these exercise tapes." The fact that the stretching and bending leaves me sore tells me that I can use some exercise myself.

Claire's eagerness to get trim was exceeded only by her desire to tan. She hardly lets a chance go by to lay out in the sun.

"How crazy," Xiao said the other day. "Girls with a dark skin color in China have trouble finding a husband."

I remembered a scene during a walk with Song where she had noticed Xiao's bronze arm next to my pale one. "Black," she had said and thrown her head back with laughter. Xiao flinched. "In the West we like a dark tan," I said, trying to rescue the situation. Yet I realized that in our country, too, racism was triggered by skin color. A tan, no matter how dark, was still a white person's tan.

Anyway, Claire wanted the brown, beach look. For five hours straight she lay on the sand or let the rays of the sun penetrate her skin as she bathed in the ocean waves. By evening she had turned red as a lobster. She tried to cool down her fiery skin by taking a cold bath, but the pain was so excruciating that she could hardly climb out of the tub. Big blisters began to form on her chest and stomach. Clothing was intolerable. By the time she had called me on the telephone for help, she was alternatingly feverish and shivering with cold. I covered her with a thick layer of first aid cream we had picked up at the clinic. Even the softest touch made her moan with pain.

"How crazy!" I agreed with Xiao. It was one thing to want a browner skin. It was another to burn herself to a crisp trying to obtain the goal.

Two days later, when Claire and I were invited to eat supper at Cao Shengli's home, Claire's blisters had started peeling but she was still barely able to sit or bend because of the sore skin on her stomach. So much for Jane Fonda exercises! Cao's Mom of course wanted to know why Claire was suddenly walking as if she had swallowed a stick. Claire wore a loose beach dress that day which hung straight down from her shoulders to minimize friction with her skin. From an oriental view point, the dress was rather risque, giving a liberal view of her shoulders and cleavage. With amazing nonchalance Claire proceeded to unbutton the dress further down to show the striking contrast of the burnt neckline and the white swell of her breast. Cao's Mom gasped and rolled her eyes. Whether it was from observing the results of Claire's torturous tanning endeavors or from shock at Claire's readiness to expose herself we will never know.

8

A Last Look

Qufu Travelogue

Traveling with three other American teachers and no Chinese translator was a new experience with some advantages and some drawbacks. Dennis and Marsha each knew enough Chinese to communicate at bus stations, hotels, and ticket counters; they loved taking over the management, so all Mona and I had to do was sit back and watch them blaze the trails. The disadvantage in this group of strong-willed adventurers was that our concepts of a successful day didn't always coincide. Mona's and Marsha's insistence on a big breakfast took two hours out of our day at Mt. Taishan because we missed the early bus. Mona and I would have liked to stay at Tai'an another day, but Dennis and Marsha wanted to return. Mona felt like taking the bus up the mountain; Marsha and I preferred climbing to the midpoint and then taking the cable car, and Dennis went all the way up on foot. To avoid disagreements, I basically stayed out of the debate and let Dennis and Marsha make the decisions.

The trip itself went more smoothly than anyone had expected. We took the 8 p.m. boat from Dalian to Yantai and watched the sunset over Dalian harbor before we settled down in a comfortable cabin for four to enjoy a short night's nap. The train left Yantai at 6:10 a.m. and got us to Yanzhou twelve hours later, early enough to catch the bus to Qufu that same evening.

Twelve hours on a train is a long time. To spend it more comfortably we upgraded our "hard seat" tickets to "hard sleeper," which got us around the smoky compartments and allowed us to take naps during the day. The waking hours were spent taking pictures from our bunk beds and philosophizing about Taoism. Dennis introduced us to Taoist religious and social thought, contrasting the nature-orientation of the Taoist with the society-orientation of the Confucians. Marsha, who is interested in traditional Chinese medicine, gave us a lecture on the Chi energy field in and around the body. I borrowed Marsha's book, *The Way of Life,* by Taoist teacher Lao Tse, which taught about yielding and humility as a way to resist destructive forces. Between reading and listening I watched the Chinese countryside: people cutting wheat with sickles; bundling them up and stacking them; carrying them to the thrashing ground; and pressing out the grain with millstones pulled by oxen, donkeys, humans, or (most rarely) small tractors. I was amazed at the wide expanse of the wheat fields. As in Kansas and Nebraska they reached to the horizon. But here each blade had been sown by hand, and harvest meant back-breaking labor.

We arrived at Qufu around 7 p.m. The town is a small out-of-the way place with a rural character. If it had not been for Confucius and his Kong family descendants, perhaps it would have disappeared amidst the wheat fields. To this day Qufu does not have a train station so that it remains off the beaten path. Nonetheless, tourism is catching hold. When we arrived everyone pointed us in the direction of the Confucian mansion where a most fancy Western-style hotel was erected just a few years ago. The bellboy in uniform received us with a cheerful "How do you do," the glass doors glided open, and we found ourselves in a sparkling reception hall. "Eighty yuan a night," they told us, and out we went. The next place looked more appropriate but turned out to be for Chinese only. "Is there no other hotel?" we asked, getting geared up for spending the night on a park bench near Confucius's tomb. Finally they gave us directions to a third place, basically for Chinese and those foreigners who can't afford tourist prices. The room had four beds and showers and toilets down the hall—for a little over three yuan a day per person. I fell asleep around midnight to the sound of a thousand croaking frogs and Marsha's steady snores.

Friday was the first real day of sightseeing. We began our tour with a visit to Confucius's temple. It was an idyllic place, alive with the song of birds and shaped by dozens of old trees. In the courtyard, way at the top of a huge old cedar, we discovered a rookery of black crown night herons.

The tombs of Confucius and his descendants were in a wooded area two miles away. My traveling companions decided to walk the stretch, while I rented a horse-drawn carriage and bounced past village scenes, gates, and booths to the edge of the burial grounds. It turned out to be a good decision to have gone ahead by myself, because this gave me time for quiet rest under the oaks and cedars. I tried to get in touch with the 2500 years of history in this place, the endless cycle of birth, learning, teaching, and dying commemorated in the tombstones among the fern. When the group arrived we went to the three burial mounds of Confucius, his son, and grandson. Dennis bowed to the great teacher, and we took all the obligatory pictures. For Marsha and Dennis, coming to Qufu had been almost a pilgrimage because they feel drawn to the old Chinese teachings. For me the place was merely restful. I could appreciate the beauty of stone-carved calligraphy, but the message remained as foreign as the philosophy itself. I plunged back into modern China by hiring a bike-drawn pedicab to take me into town.

Since Marsha and Mona wanted to nap, Dennis and I took off on our own after lunch to explore the rest of Qufu. We found another beautiful temple with twisted cedars, a turtle monument, and an exhibit of bronze-age pottery excavated nearby. Dennis rang the grass bell in the courtyard by hitting it with my wooden shoe. He woke three people up from their nap who came running to see what the problem was.

Perhaps the best experience in Qufu was a walk through the old town. On the wider streets people had spread out the freshly harvested bundles of wheat for people to walk and ride their bikes over as a convenient form of thrashing. We ran into a student of English who had come home for the weekend to help his family with the wheat harvest. After a little chat we continued our walk through a number of alleys. Though most of the homes were walled in, some of the gates stood open so that we could peek into the inner courts. We took snapshots through the gates and over the walls. Once I even talked a kind old peasant woman with bound feet into posing for a three-generation picture in front of her home with her daughter and grandchild. Dennis pointed out how the architecture of old China reflects a belief in ghosts: walls, corners, zigzag bridges, and a one-foot-high wooden board one has to step over before entering a house or temple—all those are meant to keep out evil spirits, which cannot manage to glide over steps or around corners.

Marsha and Mona joined us for a visit to the Confucian mansion, traditional home of the Kong family and a good example of a Chinese feudal landlord's residence. Near the front gate, seventh- and sixth-rank officials had once tended to taxation, legal matters, and administrative issues. Further into the complex was the living area of the Kong family with authentic furniture that had somehow managed to survive the havoc of the Cultural Revolution. Beyond the home lay a pretty Chinese garden with a goldfish pond, a zigzag bridge, a fountain, carved rocks, and twisted paths through flower beds.

The next morning we took the bus to Tai'an, a city of several million at the foot of China's holy mountain. We paid three yuan (one dollar) for a trip which lasted almost three hours and could have been advertised as a fifty-dollar scenic tour through rural China. The bus jerked over dirt roads into the remotest areas and honked its way around people pulling carts with huge loads of barrels or piles of hay. From the bus window we looked down into the backyards of poor farm homes and watched the people going about their daily chores. The horn of the bus made the most incredible trumpeting sound, like the fog horn on a ship, but the people and their beasts of burden paid little attention. They did not expect the bus to carry four curious foreigners.

In the afternoon I climbed Mount Taishan. As I look back on it now, it seems like a dream: ascending over 3,500 steps past trinket stands, pavilions, and rocks embellished with calligraphy; observing Taoist monks bring offerings of incense and food to the idols; stopping for a short rest under shaded trees; watching palm readers, juice sellers, and shopkeepers make their living through thousands of tourists who daily find their way up and down the rocky slope. Three thousand five hundred steps! How many hours of labor had it taken to carve these into the rock? Unlike the slalom turns of our mountain paths, these stairs led straight up to the summit. To the right and left amidst the trees, natural rocks covered with calligraphy offered inspiration to the weary climber who could ponder the teaching of Taoist masters while en route to the top. Unable to read Chinese, I allowed my thoughts to drift in a different direction. I realized that to complete the journey, I had to forget about the number of steps still ahead and even the stairs behind me. I needed to focus only on the very next step, then the next one, and the next. Thus the enormous climb, broken down into insignificant moves of setting one foot before the other, became a manageable task. I thought of the analogy to life: If we knew our future, would we ever have courage to tackle what lies ahead? A day at a time, we can handle what is given us.

One needs several days for Mount Taishan. We had to descend the same evening, unable to watch the sun set and rise over the mountain range. We also skipped many of the small paths to the side of the main track, and we were forced to take the cable car and bus back down rather than the picturesque western trail. But even the few hours on the mountain were filled with unforgettable moments, like my looking down on the hills of Shandong Province, or watching young girls chop stones for rock jewelry, or having a Chinese girl help me down from a steep cliff and calling me *pengyou,* "friend."

Back in the valley we waited for the midnight train amidst hundreds of sleeping bodies. Again we managed to get beds in the hard sleeper compartment. This time the train ride seemed quick because we slept through half of it. At Yantai about six hours remained until the boat's departure, so I went back to the spot on the beach that the children and I had visited several weeks ago. There were scuba divers hunting for shellfish, girls reaching for seaweed, and tourists taking pictures. I went back to the dock and relaxed, unable to absorb any more after all the impressions of the last two days. During those last hours in front of the Yantai boat dock I watched the grotesque motions of a Kung Fu artist, a blind man begging for alms, and encountered a kind old woman with a wrinkled face who invited me to drink her *qishui.*

We traveled third class on the boat because the second-class tickets were sold out. That meant we had four Chinese in the cabin with us, two men and two women, who were very surprised to discover they had Western traveling companions. Dennis told me the next morning that I must have had nightmares because I had given off a little scream. All I remembered was the Chinese man in the bunk next to mine jumping up wide-eyed and giving me a flood of Chinese words to express his concern. *"Shenme?"* ("What?") I said, still half asleep. Out came another bunch of Chinese. I rolled over and decided to ignore him. The poor fellow must have gained quite an impression of Western women!

We arrived in Dalian at 4:30 a.m., early enough for me to experience the silence of dawn and to watch the old people practice their Taiji on Zhong Shan Square. It was something I had been wanting to do for a long time. Dalian felt like home. I realized again how much I love being here and how hard it will be to leave.

Stamp Collecting

It all began with Lui Hongwei and Zhao Aiguo asking us whether we had American stamps we'd be willing to give them. Friends from Goshen had told us before we left for China that we would likely run into stamp collectors, so we had brought a small amount along.

"Why don't you come over tomorrow night," I said to Zhao, "and I'll give you some stamps. Bring friends along if you like."

Five students came that evening. I gave them most of our collection and talked about the meaning of the various stamps: statehood celebrations, black heritage, conservation, Boy Scouts, national heroes. In exchange they left us a dozen Chinese stamps.

By the next day the news had spread. Lots of students asked us to trade, and our whole supply disappeared in no time. By then Angela had caught the stamp fever. We heard from Cao Shengli that his father was a collector, so during our next visit Angela and the elder Cao withdrew in a corner of the room to study his albums. She learned that Chinese stamps were marked at the bottom to indicate the number in a particular series. Mr. Cao generously pulled duplicates for her. She proudly returned home with several dozen beautiful specimens.

To expand her collection, she knew she had to be able to trade. So we wrote to the Women's Fellowship at Akron, Indiana, asking them to send American stamps. After three weeks, a whole carton arrived. Again our student friends were the first beneficiaries, but then Angela decided it was time to join the collectors downtown.

The hub of stamp trading in Dalian is a little side alley near Tienjin Street. Every morning men of all ages gather to bargain with each other, mostly for rare and uncancelled stamps. The first time

Angela joined the crowd, she went with Song Zhihui, who helped out as a translator and watched to make sure Angela wouldn't get cheated in the transaction. They returned with such a heap of stamps that it was time to buy albums to store the treasures.

Now the fever really started raging. Angela went back almost daily, looking for new collectors she hadn't yet traded with. I accompanied her once, amazed at her nerve to mingle with the crowd. By then she had learned to bargain efficiently. She would pick a trading partner, open her little box to let him go through her collection, leaf through his albums, select the stamps she was missing in her series, and make offers. During the transaction a thick cluster of people formed around the pair, wanting to see the American girl and her method of striking a bargain. I watched from a safe distance, unable to bear having a dozen men crowd around me that closely. Angela in her determination didn't seem to mind.

There were days when we came home with only a handful of stamps, some of them torn or with missing edges. But other times she was luckier. We didn't care that much about imperfections in the stamps anyway, because the value for us was in the picture itself and the cultural content we could then discuss with our students. Among the 400 stamps she now owns, some depict scenes from famous Chinese novels; others show paintings, landscapes, Ming costumes, national heroes, New Year's lanterns, archeological finds, rare flowers, bamboo fans, musical instruments, the Eight Immortals, minority dances, Chinese opera, episodes from the "Monkey King," achievements of the working class, and of course more than a dozen portraits of Chairman Mao.

Bicycle-Hunting

One of the ways, I have discovered, to do Chinese friends a favor they will not refuse is to exchange tourists' money against Renminbi at the official 1:1 exchange rate. Most imported luxury goods and even some rare Chinese items are sold only to people with Foreign Exchange Currency. One such item is a Phoenix bicycle, sold for almost two hundred yuan (sixty-five dollars) at the Friendship Store.

So yesterday I went bicycle-hunting with Xiao. He rides his old black clunker for over an hour every day and could surely use a new one. To my surprise he laughed when I suggested replacing his bike. "I want to buy the Phoenix for my younger brother," he said. "He doesn't own any."

"Why don't you give him the old one, and you keep the new one for yourself?" I asked.

"What for? This one works fine. And my brother is young, unmarried . . . . He needs it more."

Xiao always thinks of other people. When I lent him my camera to take the first pictures of his new baby, he used part of the film for snapshots of his neighbor and child. He laughs when I tell him that was a "Christian" thing to do.

Anyway, we went to the Friendship Store only to find a sign at the main entrance which said Chinese people couldn't come in this way.

"All right, let's go to the back," I said, hiding my embarrassment. Why would they make such a rule? The side door led to the very same shopping area, and foreigners as well as Chinese were welcome as long as they paid in Foreign Exchange Currency; so why the distinction?

On the third floor we looked at some food Xiao was interested in, but another sign said that it had to be paid for in "Overseas Chinese money," whatever that is. Did they have a third type of currency I had never seen? More likely, they wanted hard currency: dollars, marks, yen.

We went on to a different section where Xiao found something he liked; but when it came time to pay, he learned that in addition to FEC, he needed a "Friendship Store Card." In other words, each Chinese person who buys there is indentifiable. The card probably has a number, which is put on the sales slip and kept, so that at any time it can be traced who bought what and how much it cost. Should the political situation ever change and China's "open door" begin to close, all those with contact to foreigners could be found out easily just because they had used Foreign Exchange Currency in the Friendship Stores. Now I realized how smart it was for Xiao to have asked me to come with him on this shopping trip. He probably anticipated that things would not go smoothly. To get around the card dilemma, I simply purchased the item myself and had Xiao pay me back.

When we got to the bike section, we saw that only one Phoenix bike was left and that it was not in good condition. Xiao read another sign announcing in Chinese that a shipment of 200 Phoenix bikes was expected any day and that customers should register for one in a nearby building. Out we went to find the place. It turned out to be a brick shack with an identical sign out in front. Two workers with bored faces sat behind an open window twiddling their thumbs. Xiao asked about the new shipment. "It came the day before yesterday," one of the men mumbled in brusque syllables. He refused to look at Xiao, indicating he would rather not be bothered.

"Can I sign up for one?" Xiao asked.

"Already sold out," came the short reply.

"Sold out in one day?"

"Yes."

"Will there be a new shipment?"

"Don't know."

We walked home. Slowly, very slowly, I regained my sense of humor. "Do you still love China?" Xiao asked with a grin. I told him that these types of difficulties were not new to me. From the beginning of our stay, I had experienced structural rigidity and bureaucratic nuisance. Simple matters were impossible to take care of because of poor management or plain reluctance to cooperate. But that didn't mean I didn't love China, because what really counted were the people: strangers who had walked up and talked to me in the streets, old women who smiled and turned their thumbs up at the sight of Stefan, students who had befriended us. Now, after the Friendship Store experience, we had even more in common. The difficulties and impossibilities were not just a nuisance for foreigners; the Chinese people themselves came up against these walls, and they had felt them all their lives. A remnant of feudal China, it forced them into a subordination with which they complied out of an instinct for survival.

Trials of a Writer

Ever since word got around that I am gathering material for a book on China, people have come with suggestions on what *they* feel ought to be written up. Cheng is enthralled with the love story of his classmate who has been seeking his advice on relational matters for the past two months. Cheng thinks this would make a wonderful romance and would give real insight into Chinese customs and ways of thinking. Perhaps it would. But it might take a Chinese to put it down on paper.

Mona wants me to capture the pathos of Chinese living in a writing style that is at once realistic and humorous. There is ample material for comedy, from the horrendous sound of people clearing their lungs and spitting in the streets to the adventure of surviving in living quarters where nothing works. Light switches are hidden behind doors or in other obscure places. The plumbing malfunctions. Electricity and water get turned off at random. The pipe under the sink is not long enough, so the dish water and food bits splatter out of the open end and miss the hole underneath. Brand-new Western-style hotels are in shambles after two or three years because no one thought of putting a vent in the bathrooms to keep mold from collecting along the walls. Because of the pollution in the cities, newly constructed housing units look like they are thirty years old in a matter of months. And on its goes. . . . But here again, do I want to write that story? What good would it do anybody? Is it right to poke fun at China simply because it has not managed to catch up with the Western world fast enough?

Claire wants me to write about a Chinese girl who had a love affair with an American and found herself isolated from the Chinese community. I am sure her story would be worth telling, because dissidents too are a part of China. I cannot deny that China has its oppressive, ugly side. But I did not experience that side personally. As a foreign teacher I was sheltered. Most of the Chinese I met were friendly, polite, and generous. Should I now go digging for the negative?

All of these proposals have merit. Perhaps all should be written up. But it might be best for Cheng just to keep counselling his friend, for Mona to laugh and cry about the haphazard living conditions, and for Claire to listen to the dissidents. Right now all I can do is describe what I see here in Dalian and reflect on what is happening to me as I seek to understand Chinese culture. I often think back to the steps of Mount Taishan and my attempt to "master the mountain" in one day. I have felt its demanding height, its fascinating lure, its seemingly ageless majesty; and I realize that, as with China, I have merely scratched the surface of all there is to learn. I don't know China or Taishan all that well, even though I can claim to have been there. Xiao sometimes half-teasingly calls me a "China expert," amused at my probing and my theories. I come and go, quickly, like a butterfly tasting the sweetness of a flower without really comprehending how the flower came to be and how it gains strength from the soil in which it is rooted. If I ever do write a book about China, it will reflect my search for understanding, not a presumption to have understood. China humbles me.

Zork

Two months before we left for China we bought a computer game called Zork. The goal is to find a treasure hidden in the depths of an underground empire. Players have to find their way through secret passages, mazes, forests, and open terrain. They encounter strange beings—some friendly, some threatening—with whom they have to communicate or at least interact in some way. To orient themselves, they are wise to make maps and take notes on paths they have chosen to explore. Often their journey ends at an unexpected impass, forcing them to start over and find another solution.

When I first played Zork, I immediately thought of the analogy with our impending China experience. We would be walking in a terrain as unknown as that of the game, puzzled by the sounds of a new language, surrounded by unintelligible signs. If a certain approach didn't work, we'd have to try another one. The goal, as in Zork, was to become as familiar as possible with the new environment; the treasure, to achieve international understanding.

Now that I have been in China, the analogy to Zork is even more striking. I vividly remember my enchantment when I first played the game. I was delighted with new discoveries and spent hours retracing my steps or exploring alternative paths. It was like a whole new world had opened up, ready to fall in my lap like a ripe plum. Then came the frustrations: going in circles, being trapped in a maze, not having tools to open a gold-encrusted egg without breaking it, being halted by an impenetrable forest. I tried again and again, using all the tools and methods I thought were available to me—but to no avail. Finally I quit playing, without ever discovering the treasure.

Looking back, I am happy that I kept a detailed journal from the beginning of our stay in China. The tone reflects the excitement of the those first weeks. Since then I have heard, and I am tempted to agree, that people coming to China often go through three stages. At first they want to write articles; a few months later they think they have enough material for a book; and finally they realize that life in China is too elusive, too complex for a Westerner to capture. Right now I begin to see the mazes, the trap doors, the impenetrable forest. How does the game of favoritism really work? Could anyone who hasn't grown up here ever understand the net of connections?

What constitutes misuse of power? How can one tell whether a friendly act is genuine or has ulterior motives? Perhaps, just as I quit playing Zork, I should quit trying to unravel China's secrets.

Claire came over earlier today with a painting from Cao Shengli and said he wanted 120 yuan for it. When we selected the work several weeks ago, Cao Shengli had hinted the price would be around 80 yuan. I feel betrayed, not because I think the picture isn't worth the 120, but because I was led to believe one thing and then it turned out otherwise. It was a replay of a disappointment I had a month ago when we went to his house under the assumption he would let us watch him paint. Instead, his mother rolled out finished pictures, looking for customers. I did not mind purchasing several of his watercolors. In fact, I was glad for the chance and have gotten much enjoyment out of the drawings. But it was unfair to rope us into something.

Somehow I no longer want the picture. I had loved it before, because it reflected the beauty and purity of China. Now it is tainted. It reminds me of frustrations and sudden little disappointments sprung upon me like a mouse trap just as I was about to eat the cheese. Yesterday afternoon, for instance, I was visiting with my students in their classroom when suddenly Wei Heping mentioned the next class would be our last together. No one from the English department had bothered to tell me! Not that I had lesson plans prepared for the rest of the month, but certainly the very last class had to be structured a bit differently. If I hadn't accidently heard from Wei Heping, I would have conducted the class as I normally do, without taking time for evaluations and good-byes. The two-hour warning at least allowed me to gather books to distribute as gifts and to bring a tape to record my students' voices.

I am overwhelmed with sadness at our life in China ending. I want to tell everyone, "Look, take it easy. We have another whole month!" But the foreign faculty are packing, and our students are getting ready for final exams. A month will be ridiculously short. "You will be coming back, won't you?" my Chinese students ask. I don't know what to say. China's open door may well close again. Even if it doesn't and I come back at some point, nothing will be the same. Xiao doesn't ask the question. He just says, "Let's not talk about it." The whole day I have felt like crying.

The First Good-bye

On Monday my advanced English class had their first final exam. Wei Heping called at lunch to tell me that right after the exam Song Zhihui had received a telegram from Tienjin that her mother-in-law had died unexpectedly. If I wanted to see Song, I should come to her room immediately.

I rushed over to the dorm and found Wei Heping waiting at the entrance. We met Song on the stairway, surrounded by a group of classmates who were going to take her to the train station. When she saw me, she started crying. I hugged her and held her tight while she told me between sobs that we probably would not meet again. We had planned to go on a ten-day trip to Shanghai, Hangzhou, and Suzhou together in July. She had been thrilled about this unique chance for her to see some of her own country, and we both were looking forward to many more hours of shared friendship. But now, in a matter of minutes, everything had changed. For Song, the loss of her mother-in-law also meant that she would not be able to come back to the Foreign Language Institute next fall, because she now had no one to take care of her two-year-old son. I grieved for Song, knowing how much she valued the opportunity to learn English and how desperately she had wanted to make up for time lost during the Cultural Revolution. Her pain and my own sorrow over our sudden separation struck me deeply. We cried together, right in front of all these Chinese classmates who must have been stunned at our emotional parting. How could we have grown so close over these past few weeks? "I will never forget you, never!" said Song, and I believed her. There was no more time, not even to write down her address or mine. The others surrounded her again and took her down the stairs past the English Department. She turned around to me again, looking pale and distraught. Around her neck I saw the little golden heart pendant I had given her three days before. At least there had been time to give each other little tokens. . . .

Travel Plans

The date for our departure is drawing near. Final exams in Chinese are on July 7; the BCA students leave the next day, and with their departure our responsibility as program directors ends. We have our flight booked from Hongkong for July 29, and we'll spend the last three weeks in China sightseeing.

A tour through the coastal cities should be fun and exciting, but to us it sounds more and more like an endurance test. First of all, we will have to put up with scorching heat. While China's elite flocks north to places like Dalian to catch a cool ocean breeze, we'll be roasting in crowded southern urban centers. Next, there is the hassle with luggage. Even if we ship two of our suitcases to Hongkong, we are still left with our portable computer, two violins, and the rest of the luggage we'll need for three weeks en route. Carrying things in and out of train stations is a pain, and storing them in the luggage room is risky. Third, we have the language problem. Although Ken now knows basic conversational Chinese, the pronunciation varies from province to province. And for managers of restaurants and hotels it is an advantage not to understand, because that way they can charge higher prices. How will we find a good place to stay? How can we keep from being cheated? Who will help us get to the sights we want to visit?

We thought one solution to these problems would be to invite a student from the Institute to accompany us. But that leads to a different set of complications. If we ask for a specific person, the authorities will be suspicious that the student sought to befriend us for some kind of personal advantage. On the trip itself, hotels for foreigners would be off-limits for our guide; and we in turn would not be allowed to stay in Chinese hotels. Even restaurants are segregated at times. So the student might have to find food and housing on her own. And she would have to travel back to Dalian all by herself after we have left Southern China. . . .

Every now and then, in our some pessimistic moments, we wonder whether it wouldn't be better just to stay in Dalian until the end of July. But Ken wants to see the Great Wall, and I am dreaming of Suzhou's miraculous gardens, Shanghai's jade buddha,

Hangzhou's West Lake, and Guangzhou's markets. If we ever want to visit those sights, now is the time. I am sure we will learn a lot about China! Maybe in the midst of all the hassle of booking train tickets and being overcharged in restaurants, hotels, and tour buses we will meet some Chinese people with good will and enough English language skills to show us around.

Time to Go

A new Japanese family with children is moving in this afternoon, and we have agreed to vacate our apartment to make room for them. We only heard about this two days ago, in typcial Chinese administrative style. So we have been packing rather frantically. Actually, it suits me fine to get the suitcases ready six days in advance, because there will be so many other last-minute details to take care of. However, this also means packing up the computer. No more writing until we get to North Manchester!

The last two weeks have passed quickly. Our classes asked us to join them for photographing sessions. Students stopped by with little souvenirs for us. We took friends out to dinner, visited places in Dalian for maybe the last time, and slowly got used to the idea of leaving. I met with Xiao almost daily. He wrote out Chinese phrases for me that I can point to during our three-week tour to express what I want in restaurants, train stations, and hotels. As we walked through Dalian we talked about everything under the sun, and I realized with gratitude what a rare friendship we have—even by Western standards, let alone for a foreigner in China. Our meetings now stand more and more under the shadow of having to part soon. We are both realistic enough to know that I will likely not come back, that he can't leave, and that letter-writing will dwindle, perhaps even cease. I am preparing vigorously for the trip through China to distract myself from the pain of separating.

Home Again?

A whole month has passed since my last journal entry. We are back in the States after an eventful three weeks of traveling through China. Returning to North Manchester has provoked emotions similar to those when we first arrived in Dalian. We marvel at the differences between the two cultures and make new discoveries that we would never have perceived if we had stayed home the last six months. I want to record my first impressions before life here becomes routine again and we no longer notice what now surprises us.

Everyone looks pale in Indiana, even people with a tan. I miss the golden faces of Asia. Some of our friends have a whitish-pink complexion that looks almost anemic. It feels like I have never seen so many blond-haired individuals in my life.

Strangers no longer stare. We get attention from those who have known us and are welcoming us back, but everyone else is understandably indifferent. Stefan, who at times deeply resented being pawed and stroked and kissed by people he had never met, now craves hugs from Mom to compensate for what he has lost.

In contrast, I myself feel perplexed by the many friendly embraces by male acquaintances who are welcoming us back. After half a year in a culture where men and women don't touch each other unless they are engaged or married, and where a kiss in public would be considered scandalous even for married couples, I need to relearn the pattern of expressing affection physically and casually. It seems as if it were yesterday that I parted from Xiao who had become such a close friend. How easy it would have been, in a Western context, to give him a good-bye hug! But we just stood there and never even took each other's hand. In China, affection is transmitted only through eye contact. I like the physical freedom to touch people, but I will miss the subtlety and depth of emotion that I sensed in the relationships with my Chinese friends.

It was strange to wake up in North Manchester. We had attempted to stay up late the night before; but because of the fourteen-hour time change we still awoke at 5 a.m. and couldn't get back to sleep. All around us was silence except for the crickets in the surrounding lawns. At that early hour I didn't expect too much noise, but by 6 a.m. I caught myself listening to the sounds of Dalian waking up: people talking on their way to work, traffic moving past, cars honking, construction workers dropping their heavy loads. But North Manchester remained deadly quiet. Only a few birds chirped in the trees. Around 10 a.m. Stefan and I went for a walk to rediscover our neighborhood. Still, there was not a sound except for an occasional dog barking. The streets seemed deserted, the houses empty. In Dalian, as in any other Chinese city, one could not step out of a building without seeing people. Walking down the street meant joining hundreds of pedestrians, jumping aside at the honk of a truck or bus, and making way for dozens of bicycles trying to squeeze through the crowds, slalom fashion. North Manchester seemed like a ghost town.

Astonishingly enough, our house impressed me as smaller than I had remembered it. Because of the crowded quarters in China, my mind had created an image of an absolutely huge living-dining room area and many spacious rooms. I was relieved to find that, although spacious by Chinese standards, the house was relatively humble.

One of the delightful surprises of being back in the United States was the ability to understand everyone. Not that we had expected it to be otherwise; but we had grown accustomed to having to express ourselves in a difficult language and being surrounded all day long by sounds and written messages we could seldom comprehend.

Another thing I appreciated was the striking beauty and cleaniness of the towns and the general landscape. China, in its urgency to catch up with the more developed nations, has not paid much attention to ecology. Overflowing trash bins, stinky public latrines, air pollution from factories, impure water, cans and paper tossed carelessly into the street, beaches covered with broken glass . . . all those images come back to mind. Here I can use a public toilet without having to hold my breath. The streets look immaculate. I have not seen anyone spitting. And when I turn on the water faucet, I remind myself each time, "Yes, indeed, you can drink this. It doesn't need to be boiled."

An unpleasant surprise was the cost of living. We paid sixty-three dollars on our first trip to the grocery store to stock up on some basic necessities. In Dalien, grocery bills seldom exceeded ten yuan, or three dollars; cucumbers cost three cents per pound. The level of consumption here is amazing. On the other hand, at least as far as nutrition is concerned, we look forward to changing our diet of rice and fungus soup to more balanced meals.

Perhaps the most striking change between Dalien and North Manchester is the pace of living. We were barely home for two days when we found it necessary to pull out our date books to keep track of upcoming appointments. The "things to do" list grew by the hour. Gone was the relaxed attitude of dealing with life as it happened from day to day. We were back to deadlines, commitments, and the crazy Western compulsion of having to "manage time." In China it seemed disconcerting to be out of control; now it seems an obsession to want to be *in* control. How funny people are! Am I glad to be home? It's hard to say. Perhaps I am . . . but China is still part of me. For six months, it too was "home." As global citizen I will always remain a little homesick for the rest of the world.

A Last Look

Stefan Rogers with an older Chinese friend

Angela Rogers with Chinese students at the seashore

Children waiting to sing and dance for a Children's Day *performance*

The tomb of Confucius

Studying for a performance of Our Town

Stefan Rogers and Chinese students

*An English
conversation class*

Trading stamps

*Stefan watching
an artist at work*

*Angela learning
to make* jiaozi,
*pockets of dough
stuffed with vegetables
and meat and
steamed*

Readers please sign   1991

Willie Ellis
Marcella Wieland April 1992
Regina Barrington July 1992